BRIAN

SENT FORTH

BRIAN MᶜCALLUM

Ministering
Spirits

SENT FORTH

23 22 21 20 19 18 17   07 06 05 04 03 02 01

Ministering Spirits Sent Forth
ISBN-13: 978-0-89276-935-3
ISBN-10: 0-89276-935-1

In the U.S. write:
Kenneth Hagin Ministries
P.O. Box 50126
Tulsa, OK 74150-0126
1-888-28-FAITH
rhema.org

In Canada write:
Kenneth Hagin Ministries of Canada
P.O. Box 335, Station D
Etobicoke (Toronto), Ontario
Canada M9A 4X3
1-866-70-RHEMA
rhemacanada.org

CONTENTS

INTRODUCTION

Since Jesus Christ became the Lord of my life in 1964, I have experienced wonderful instances of angelic protection, deliverance, prosperity, and fruitfulness in ministry.

However, that is not where God's angels began to work in my life. To this day I do not fully know or realize how they ministered for me even before my salvation, which occurred when I was 32 years old.

The Lord has been gracious not only to send angels to minister for me in those years when I was unsaved but also to reveal to me in subsequent years what they had done to preserve my life in peacetime, Cold War, and hot war from all the devices that Satan had formed against me.

Let me say at this point that the prayers of previous generations of my family, other precious saints used of the Lord, my wife, my children, and myself have been and are still being marvelously answered according to their and our faith in His Word.

Many times the answer to the saints' prayers have come through angels ministering for us. You will read of many in this book.

I am eternally grateful to God for His grace in Christ Jesus and for the gift of faith whereby we partake of that grace. In the very important time in which we live, we will witness the testimony of Revelation 6:13.

REVELATION 6:13
13 And the stars of heaven [a symbolic term for angels] fell unto the earth, even as a fig tree casteth her untimely figs, when she is shaken of a mighty wind [like the mighty wind of Acts 2:2].

This is speaking of a great increase in angelic activity in the earth which can only be in response to a great increase of believers living and speaking the Word of God to commission the angels to do God's commandments in the earth. I already see that increase happening today in the church of Jesus Christ.

This book will help all of us take our place and fulfill our responsibility so that the Lord of hosts, Jehovah Sabaoth, can direct us all to the ripening of the number of the elect and the fulfilling of all His plans and purposes for the saints and for this world in which we are light and salt.

Brian K. McCallum

Broken Arrow, Oklahoma

HOW ANGELS WORK ON YOUR BEHALF

This book will be a search of the scriptures concerning God's angels. Angels have a good report in the Word of God, and you will like what you read about angels. You will learn some things angelic beings have been doing for you for a long time, even though you may not have been aware of their actions.

That's the way it has been in my own Christian walk. As I have grown in the knowledge of God, I have also grown in my knowledge and understanding of the working of angels.

In this book, you will learn that *we have a part to play in receiving the ministry of angels.* Our part in being able to receive this ministry is similar to the part we play in having dominion in the earth concerning demons and fallen angels. This dominion hinges on our being submitted to God. *Good things don't happen to us unless we are submitted to God.*

The ministry of angels is one of the subjects I most enjoy teaching from the Word of God, because I understand what the ministry of angels has done for me personally. The most important thing was that the ministry of angels kept me alive when I wasn't saved. *Angels kept me alive to get saved.*

HEBREWS 1:14
14 Are they [angels] not all ministering spirits, sent forth to minister *for* them who shall be heirs of salvation?

Some will say, "Why did they do that for you and not for everyone else?" You will learn the answer to this as we go along, but it is simply because God has foreknowledge. Often God gives people an unction to pray for you, and thereby He also commissions angels to work on your behalf even before you are saved and learn you have a call on your life.

What God says about those of us who are born again is true:

HEBREWS 12:22–24

22 But ye are come unto mount Sion, and unto the city of the living God, the
heavenly Jerusalem, and to an innumerable company of angels.

23 To the general assembly and church of the firstborn, which are written in
heaven, and to God the Judge of all, and to the spirits of just men made
perfect.

24 And to Jesus the mediator of the new covenant, and to the blood of sprinkling, that speaketh better things than that of Abel.

This passage speaks of those who have come to Jesus Christ—those
who are born again, regenerated, and living in the kingdom of God. We
have come to every blessing in God's kingdom.

PILGRIMS ON THE EARTH

Remember, our citizenship is always primarily in Heaven. No
matter where our citizenship is on earth, that's secondary. The Word
of God even calls us "pilgrims" in this world. We are passing through
it, but we are not of it. We are in it, but we are no longer of it. Our
citizenship and our connections are primarily to God in the kingdom
of God. We are His children. He is our Father.

This truth is described in symbolic language in the above passage.
Verse 22 says we have come to "Mount Zion." When we got saved, we
didn't take a ship, cross the Atlantic Ocean into the Mediterranean, sail
down to the other end of that sea, disembark, climb up a hill in Israel,
and say, "Save me, Lord." That's not where most of us got saved. We
were not physically in Israel, where Mount Zion is located, when we
got saved.

LIVING IN HEAVEN

But we came to the *heavenly* Mount Zion. We came to the kingdom
of God. That's what the phrase means. We were born into God's kingdom, the kingdom of Heaven. So when we came to Christ, we came to
Mount Zion, the city of the living God, the heavenly Jerusalem. That
is our eternal city.

We are already living in Heaven! We are born into the kingdom of God, and in that kingdom there is an "innumerable" company of angels, according to verse 22. I don't know how many "innumerable" is, and you don't, either, but I do know it is more than enough. If you needed a whole host of angels, you would have all you needed, and we often do need them.

According to Jeremiah 33:22, there are more angels than can be counted; more than man can grasp with his finite knowledge. *"The host of heaven cannot be numbered"* it says.

Therefore, when we came to Mount Zion, the City of the Living God, by virtue of our new birth—by being born into the kingdom of Heaven—we also came to a place where there is an innumerable company of angels and the general assembly and the Church of the Firstborn.

That is who we are in the world today: We are the general assembly. We are the Church of the Firstborn whose names are written in Heaven. We came to God through Christ, and we were united with Him, the Judge of all, and to *"the spirits of just men made perfect."*

"JUST MEN MADE PERFECT"

The human beings in Heaven are there *spiritually*; however, their bodies are not yet there. Having finished their course and their race and having died a natural death, they have gone to be with the Lord. Their spirits and souls are in that kingdom, and they will be reunited with their bodies at the resurrection.

We read in Hebrews 12:1 that we are surrounded by a great host of these witnesses in Heaven.

HEBREWS 12:1
1 Wherefore seeing we also are compassed about with so great a cloud of witnesses.

They are the spirits of the just men (and women) made perfect, mentioned in verse 23.

Verse 24 speaks of *"Jesus the mediator of the new covenant."* Jesus is who? The Word of God. In the beginning was the Word, the Word was with God, and the Word was God.

We came to all this when we were born again: to Jesus the mediator of the new covenant and to Jesus' blood of sprinkling that speaks of life, deliverance, safety, preservation, and everything else that salvation is to us. As verse 24 notes, that blood still speaks better things to us today than that of Abel.

There are three that always agree, First John 5:8 says: (1) *the Spirit,* (2) *the water (Word),* and (3) *the blood.* The Spirit of God says the same thing that the blood speaks. The blood speaks the same thing that the Word of God promises. They are always in agreement.

GOD'S PLANS AND PURPOSES

The purpose of angelic ministry is to carry out the plans and purposes of the Godhead. Remember that song we used to sing: "God Rides on Wings of Love." That was a good song. We should sing songs like that today. We don't need to discard good scriptural songs. Truth is truth, and truth stays true; it doesn't change. God rides on wings of love.

There are references in the Word to angelic hosts, chariots of God, and innumerable thousands of angels. God accomplishes His purposes through the ministry of this angelic host and these angelic beings. They see to it that God's Word comes to pass.

Someone will say, "I'm a man of God. It's just me and God. We don't need any help." But what if God intended for you to receive help through the ministry of angels? Would it be all right then if you received help that way? If God provided help through angels, it's all right to receive it that way, isn't it?

CHARACTERISTICS OF ANGELIC MINISTRY

An important characteristic of angelic ministry is that *it always glorifies the Lord Jesus Christ.* There will never be a time when

Jesus isn't the central figure in what angels do. Of course, we're considering godly angelic ministry. There are other angels—fallen angels—that appear in different ways, but they don't glorify Jesus in anything they do.

Furthermore, *angelic ministry always agrees with the Word.* God has made it so simple. If it glorifies Jesus, it has to agree with the Word.

Angelic ministry always agrees with and is centered on the Word of God. It won't leave you wondering whether it's a godly angel or not. There will be no doubt in your mind.

Angelic ministry is always right in the "middle of the road" as far as agreeing with the Word. It isn't "far out." You will always plainly see agreement with the Word of God when angels are at work. They don't leave you scratching your head and wondering.

Some will argue, "We need some of those 'far-out' things." No, you don't need something that's farther out than the Word of God! Because angelic ministry is always in agreement with the Word of God, that makes it exciting. Getting beyond the Word is not exciting.

"NEW" MAY BE WRONG

Once at a large meeting I heard a preacher say something, and the crowd gave him the loudest shout I'd ever heard. But what he said was *wrong*! Most of those people were Christians. Why did they all shout so loud? Because the preacher said something they had never heard before!

People have a tendency to get excited and stirred up in the flesh over something new. You can always find plenty of things that are new to you in the Word. There is always something new in Christ. The mercies of God are new every morning, for one thing. If you want to get excited, get excited about that.

What that speaker said was totally wrong. Why was he invited to be a speaker? I don't know, but everyone thought his message was exciting because it was different and new. However, you should bear in mind that "new and different" teachings are not always necessarily in agreement with the Word of God.

JESUS AND ANGELS

John tells us how important it is that angelic ministry always agrees with and is centered on the Word of God. You will see the emphasis Jesus Himself put on the ministry of angelic beings. For example, He said to Nathanael:

JOHN 1:51
51 Verily, verily, I say unto you, Hereafter ye shall see heaven open, and the angels of God ascending and descending upon the Son of man.

In fact, we find several references in the Gospels where angels of God ministered to Jesus' needs. *They ministered to Him because He was a real human being.* He needed their ministry. You and I need it, too. If Jesus needed it, think how much more *we* need it!

In the first chapter of John, we find where Jesus went forth in Galilee and started choosing His disciples. He called them to follow Him, as we see in this passage.

JOHN 1:43–46
43 The day following Jesus would go forth into Galilee, and findeth Philip, and saith unto him, Follow me.
44 Now Philip was of Bethsaida, the city of Andrew and Peter.
45 Philip findeth Nathanael, and saith unto him, We have found him, of whom Moses in the law, and the prophets, did write, Jesus of Nazareth, the son of Joseph.
46 And Nathanael said unto him, Can there any good thing come out of Nazareth? Philip saith unto him, Come and see.

"COME AND SEE!"

When some people find out where you come from, they may say the same thing about you, wondering if anything good can come out of *your* hometown! Answer them the same way Philip answered Nathanael: "Come and see. See for yourself!"

Didn't we see Jesus? Philip and Nathanael saw how good Jesus was. We saw His grace. We beheld it because the grace of God enabled us to see it. "Come and see" for yourself!

JOHN 1:47
47 Jesus saw Nathanael coming to him, and saith of him, Behold an Israelite indeed, in whom there is no guile!

I take that statement to mean not that Nathanael was perfect, but that his heart was set on keeping the Mosaic covenant by faith, not religiously like the Pharisees, the Sadducees, and many others in those groups. Nathanael was trusting God for his salvation, and he, like Simeon, Anna, and other righteous persons, was expecting the Messiah to come.

"I SAW THEE"

JOHN 1:48
48 Nathanael saith unto him, Whence knowest thou me? Jesus answered and said unto him, Before that Philip called thee, when thou wast under the fig tree, I saw thee.

Jesus had a word of knowledge about what Nathanael had been doing under that fig tree! It seems he was seeking God, because he readily recognized who Jesus was when He described what He saw. Nathanael wanted to know the Messiah. He was longing after Him. And when he saw Him, he recognized Him!

JOHN 1:48–49
48 Nathanael answered and saith unto him, Rabbi, thou art the Son of God; thou art the King of Israel.
49 Jesus answered and said unto him, Because I said unto thee, I saw thee under the fig tree [because you saw something supernatural, because you recognized I knew something about you] believest thou? thou shalt see greater things than these.

SEEING THE KINGDOM OPEN

Now Jesus is going to describe what He is talking about, and He is also going to show us something concerning those three statements we made about the angelic ministry.

JOHN 1:51

> 51 And he saith unto him, Verily, verily, I say unto you, Hereafter ye shall see heaven open, and the angels of God ascending and descending upon the Son of man.

Except when Nathanael passed out of this life, I don't necessarily think he ever saw Heaven. He may have had visions of Heaven—he may have been caught away like others have been—the Bible doesn't say he did. But I know he saw something that Jesus is referring to here: He saw the kingdom of Heaven opened to him, just like you and I have seen the kingdom of Heaven opened to us.

I personally have never gone up to Heaven. I have never been caught up to Heaven. I haven't stood in Heaven and seen what some people have seen in Paradise, but I don't doubt for a minute that it's all true the way the Bible says it is.

However, I have seen the kingdom of Heaven opened to me. Everyone who is born again has seen the kingdom of Heaven opened to him or her.

UNDERSTANDING SPIRITUAL THINGS

Nevertheless, for the first six years after it was opened to me, I didn't see much of it, because I wasn't in the Word. In the Word of God you see what is opened to you. That's where the reality of Heaven becomes real to you. That's where the reality of your new birth takes hold. That's where Jesus begins to teach you all about Who He is, what this kingdom is all about, and how it operates.

Do you remember the day Jesus' disciples asked Him, "Why do You speak in parables? Why don't You just say things plainly?" (Matt. 13:10–11). He replied, "Because it is given to you to know how the kingdom of Heaven operates." They must have been able to spiritually understand the parables He gave at that time.

Jesus said the people of the world could not understand the parables, but believers could. Therefore, He spoke in parables because we are able to discern and understand them; and if we have questions about them, we ought to ask the same Person His disciples asked.

When Jesus taught the parable of the wheat and the tares, His disciples asked Him to explain it, and He did. He explained it in plain language to them. He still does this through the Spirit of Truth in us.

HELPED BY THE SPIRIT OF TRUTH

If we have questions about anything written symbolically in the Word of God and we can't grasp it immediately with our human understanding, the Lord will explain it to us, because the Spirit of Truth is in us, and He can explain it to us.

That's why Jesus said to His disciples, *"Unto you it is given to know the mysteries of the kingdom of God"* (Matt. 13:11). God wants us to know how His kingdom works and how we receive its blessings living in the kingdom.

That's why Jesus said to Nathanael, *"Hereafter ye shall see heaven open, and the angels of God ascending and descending upon the Son of man"* (John 1:51).

You won't necessarily see the third Heaven, but all who seek will see how the kingdom of Heaven operates and will understand that they are living in a kingdom with angelic beings.

WHO IS "THE SON OF MAN"?

Who is the "Son of man" mentioned in this verse? Who else but the Word of God! Actually, when you see the term "Son of man," that's the closest term for the Word of God. Jesus used that name to refer to Himself over and over again.

He was referring to His own humanity and to the fact that His humanity was anointed, and He, as the Son of man, had appeared to man to reveal Himself as the Word of God (John 1:14).

He was God forever. And when He submitted Himself in the God-head to become the Savior of mankind even before He was manifested as the Son of man He was the Word of God. He has always been that, but He didn't initially manifest Himself outwardly as God on earth.

Coming God's Way

Jesus walked this earth as the Son of man first to do the work of salvation so we would recognize Him as being the Son of God as well as the Son of man. He still manifests Himself to everyone who believes.

He had to do it that way to fulfill all righteousness so He would not come unjustly into this world and force anything to happen. He had to come God's way to bring the whole work of salvation to pass.

By laying down His life as a man, He saved us. By shedding His blood as a human being, He died for us. He took on Himself the nature of Abraham or mankind in order to save us. He didn't take on Himself the nature of angels; instead, He became a human being so He might die for us (Heb. 2:9).

He told Nathanael, "You will see the angels of God ascending and descending upon the Word of God." You could say it that way. Certainly, angels did minister to Jesus. We read in several places in the Gospels that angels ministered to His human need, but that is not what He is referring to here.

Commissioning Angels

Instead, He is referring to the fact that you will see the ministry of angels centered on, responding to, and being commissioned by people who live in the Word of God and speak it from their hearts.

If you live in the Word, you will see the ministry of angels. You will see Heaven opened, and you will see angels ascending and descending upon that Word, centered on that Word, keeping that Word, and bringing that Word to pass.

There is another place in scripture where someone heard a similar statement. It was Jacob. He'd had a difference of opinion with his brother, Esau. Their mother was concerned that Esau was so enraged with Jacob, he would kill him. Therefore, she sent Jacob to her brother, Laban, back in Padanaram. Jacob obeyed. We find this story in Genesis 28:10–12.

GENESIS 28:10–12
10 And Jacob went out from Beersheba and went toward Haran.
11 And he lighted upon a certain place,and tarried there all night, because the sun was set; and he took of the stones of that place and put them for his pillows, and lay down in that place to sleep.
12 And he dreamed....

SEEING INTO THE KINGDOM

In dreams and visions, we see into the kingdom. Jacob dreamed, *"and behold a ladder set up on the earth, and the top of it reached to heaven"* (v. 12).

This is symbolic. You don't see a ladder anywhere on the earth that reaches all the way to Heaven. You can walk all over this earth, from the North Pole to the South Pole and everywhere in between, and you won't find any such ladder. But it does symbolize something that is more true than anything you could see with your natural eyes.

GENESIS 28:12
12 The top of it reached to heaven: and behold the angels of God ascending and descending on it.

This is something the Word of God does that connects Heaven and earth.

You are born into the kingdom of God. You are seated spiritually in heavenly places in Christ Jesus, but you are also seated somewhere on earth reading this book right now. You are there because you are human. You are still in this world, although you are not of it, and you need to overcome while you live in it.

CONNECTING THE KINGDOMS

Therefore, a connection needs to be made for you between the kingdom where you are seated in the heavenly places and the natural world where you live. *That connection is the angelic ministry.* That connection has everything to do with angelic ministry. Jesus made it for you, and there is a definite connection between the two kingdoms.

Angels affect many things in the natural realm on your behalf. They will change things in this natural world according to your faith in God's Word to meet your need. We see some of these things mentioned in Genesis chapter 28.

The ladder reached to Heaven, and the angels of God ascended and descended on it. In John's Gospel we see the angels of God ascending and descending upon the Word of God, the Son of man. When this happens for you, you will recognize it one of two ways. You may see it with your natural eyes, or you will more often perceive it with your spirit, by spiritual gift, dream, vision, or plain faith in God's Word.

Seeing in the Spirit

Sometimes it's a dream, like Jacob had. His eyes were closed—he was asleep—and he saw it by his spirit. He was seeing from God's view. Sometimes we see things that way, but we will see it by revelation in our spirit, whether we see it internally or externally.

Sometimes you will literally see angels. They will appear to you. Sometimes you will see them with your senses and recognize that they are appearing to you. Sometimes you won't see them with your senses, but you will recognize they are doing their job. At other times, they will appear as natural human beings and do something for you, but you won't immediately recognize it was an angel!

GENESIS 28:13
13 And, behold, the Lord stood above it.

In Jacob's day, Jesus was not yet manifested as the Son of man, so when He appeared in the earth, He came as the angel of the Lord. He appeared to people, ministered to them, did things for them, and told them certain truths. Again, because Jesus was not yet manifested as the Son of man, the Word of God was not yet revealed in the measure it is today.

THE PROMISED INHERITANCE

GENESIS 28:13

13 And, behold, the Lord stood above it, and said, I am the Lord God of Abraham thy father, and the God of Isaac: the land whereon thou liest, to thee will I give it, and to thy seed.

The land upon which Jacob lay was still part of the covenant land God had promised to Abraham and Isaac, and that promise was good to Jacob. It was fulfilled to their descendants after they came out of Egypt.

Even though Jacob and his twelve sons lived in the land and were blessed and profited by living there, it was never theirs. It wasn't Abraham's or Isaac's, either, but they were always welcomed and blessed by it. People favored them in it, yet the land did not became Israel's by possession until *after* the Exodus of the Jewish people from Egypt.

ALL OF GOD'S PROMISES

The land was the Jewish people's promise from God. It summarized all God had promised to do for that nation. But you and I have a promise that is much greater than just a piece of territory. *Our promise is the sum of all of God's promises!* They are all "yea and amen" to us in Christ.

Therefore, when we look at that word "land," we see that God promised to lead the Jews into their land, give it to them, and protect and bless them there. We understand it means everything to us that the Word promises us. The whole Bible is "yea and amen" to us in Christ!

So if you want some land, ask God. He will give you some. But that is not the extent of what He can do for you. Remember, when you get your land, you are going to have to be a good steward of it, so ask wisely. Don't get more land than you can take care of.

THE RESULT OF JACOB'S FAITH

GENESIS 28:13–14

13 The land whereon thou liest, to thee I will give it, and to thy seed;

14 And thy seed shall be as the dust of the earth, and thou shalt spread abroad to the west, and to the east, and to the north, and to the south: and in thee and in thy seed shall all the families of the earth be blessed.

That is a direct promise from Christ, isn't it? It is a direct promise of the Gospel coming not only to this nation of Israel but also to the whole world. The whole world will be blessed because of Jacob's faith. The whole world will be blessed by that godly line that will produce Jesus Christ the Word of God, the Son of man, and the Son of God in the earth.

So the Lord said to Jacob, "All the earth will be blessed, and you will spread out over the whole earth," but the Jewish nation never did that. Who will spread out over the whole earth and fulfill that prophecy? The Church will. With what? The Gospel of Jesus Christ!

HELPED BY ANGELS

Although they will not do it for us, angels will help us spread the Gospel around the world. Our part is to go and preach, and when we do this, they will go with us. And when they go with us, they will make all kinds of wonderful, divine connections for us to accomplish our job. For example, they will bring people to us who are seeking to know the truth, and they will see to it that we succeed wherever we go.

I have gone to places where the Gospel had never been preached. When our team arrived, we found those people were bound by demonic forces. We could just sense that there was a lot of demonic activity in that place.

When it was time for us to hold a meeting and preach, a huge crowd assembled to hear the truth, and it seemed like the whole host of Heaven flew through there and "charged" the atmosphere, changing it from the way it had been when we arrived and bringing light to a land that was in great darkness.

Angels help you do what God sent you to do. They are there to help you. They are there to minister for you. And one of the things they want to help you do is accomplish whatever God told you to do.

This is the first general area in which angels minister for and in us. Why? Because God wants us to be a light to this world and salt to this earth. He wants us to spread out over the whole earth.

THE KEEPING POWER OF GOD

God said further to Jacob in verse 15:

GENESIS 28:15
15 And behold, I am with thee, and will keep thee in all places whither thou goest and will bring thee again into this land: for I will not leave thee.

"Keeping" implies more than just spiritual keeping. Thank God, you are kept spiritually by grace; thank God, you are saved by grace; and, thank God, you are assured by grace. Thank God for the keeping power of God to keep you in the way, which is in Christ. But you need to be kept more than that.

PSALM 103:1–2
1 Bless the Lord, O my soul: and all that is within me, bless his holy name.
2 Bless the Lord, O my soul, and forget not all of his benefits.

This keeping power is part of the benefits, and you are to be mindful of them. In doing so, God will keep you not only spiritually but naturally. That Psalm goes on to say in verse 4 that God will even redeem your life from destruction.

ANGELS SPRING SATAN'S TRAPS

There is an enemy out there—the devil—who wants to steal, kill, and destroy you. But angelic beings will guard you from it. The devil will work for twenty years to set a trap for you, but before you put your foot in it, the angels will spring it!

It must be frustrating for the devil. Truthfully, I'm sure he must be the most frustrated being in the universe. But I'm not sorry for him; he deserves everything he got. He purchased everything he has. It's his own desire, his own will, and now he's got it.

He can't do one thing to the person who realizes where and who he is in Christ. When you walk in this world naturally, even though the devil is the god of this world for this age and is able to do things through unbelieving people and set traps for people, God will protect you from these things.

Walking in an Alien World

You are walking around in an alien world. The world system is against you. The devil is against you. Often your own flesh and blood doesn't agree with you. God will keep you from the effects of these things, but you have a role to play in believing and receiving His help. God promised He will keep you in all places you go. When your way is His way, He will keep you in it.

As we read in Genesis 28:15, God promised, *"I am with thee, and will keep thee in all places whither thou goest, and will bring thee again into this land"* or into all your inheritance.

Receiving Your Inheritance

This is an area we need to examine. God said the angels will help you receive your inheritance! Since this is so, we need to understand how they will do it.

I believe God for substance. I believe angels are at work to bring me whatever money or things I may need. Angels will contact this world on your behalf, too, to bring you that substance, and they can even influence the world to give it to you!

God can influence and move the Church if its members will let Him, but God can go a lot further than what the Church can give you. God, not the Church, is your source. This world is God's, and the fullness of it belongs to Him. Although a great deal of that fullness is presently in the hands of unbelieving people, God can cause the angels to bring what you need out of the hands of unbelieving people and under your control. God truly is the Lord of hosts.

It is the angels who do it for you. Something must contact that natural world and deliver it to you. You can't make it happen. No man can make it happen—but God can. And His *angels are the means by which God provides you with power and provision!*

"THE LORD IS IN THIS PLACE"

GENESIS 28:16

16 And Jacob awaked out of his sleep, and he said, Surely the Lord is in this place; and I knew it not.

Sunday mornings at 11 o'clock, many people can say that, and they won't be kidding. The church I went to as I was growing up had a sign out in front that read, "Worship at 11 o'clock." At 11 o'clock we were doing everything but that!

We never worshipped, because we didn't know what worship was. We didn't know what praise was, either. We gathered more or less as a social group. I don't know what the angels did around that kind of church. I don't suppose there were a lot of them there.

GENESIS 28:16–17

16 Jacob . . . said, Surely the Lord is in this place; and I knew it not.
17 And he was afraid, and said, How dreadful is this place!

How awesome—not terrible or terrorizing him—but how awesome was that place to Jacob. He went on to say, *"This is none other but the house of God and this is the gate of heaven."*

JESUS: JACOB'S LADDER

Jacob recognized that the Ladder he saw was the connection between him and God; a connection made for his benefit.

And who is the Ladder? Jesus! He is the bridge over troubled waters. He is the Ladder on which the angels of God ascend and descend.

It is the Word of God (Jesus) that will see to it that God's Word is kept, and it is the Word of God that angels operate on, right in the middle of it.

As we saw, Psalm 103 speaks of not forgetting all of God's benefits. It speaks of how He will forgive all your iniquities, heal all your diseases, redeem your life from destruction, crown you with loving-kindness and tender mercies, and satisfy your mouth with good things.

We might understand the latter phrase as referring to food. I'm sure what goes into your mouth gives that impression. God will satisfy you with good food. The Bible says God did this for Israel, and He will do it for you and me. When you pray over your food, He does bless it and makes it good meat for your flesh.

YOU CAN HAVE WHAT YOU SAY

However, there is something far more important than food that goes into your mouth. It is what comes *out* of your mouth. God satisfies your mouth with good things. The world walks around saying negative, nasty, ugly things, and they get what they say.

But God satisfies your mouth with good things, and you can have what you say. What you say and do in response to what you say has everything to do with what angels can do for you.

In Psalm 103, we read:

PSALM 103:20
20 Bless the Lord, ye his angels, that excel in strength, that do his commandments, hearkening unto the voice of his word.

Who gives voice to God's Word today? Believers do in the earth. God doesn't do it for you; you do it. God helps by enabling you to do it, but you are the one who speaks the Word of God in the earth today. You have dominion in the earth. It was given to you by Jesus, the Head of the Church (Matt. 28:18).

GIVING VOICE TO GOD'S WORD

So when you speak the Word of God, angels hearken to it. The Word commissions an angel or angels—whatever the need may be—to minister for you. You commission them by believing and acting on the Word of God.

No one believes the Word of God without believing it in his heart and speaking it with his mouth. No one is a believer without acting on the Word of God.

So when you believe, speak, and act according to what you know, you commission angelic beings, and they go forth and act on your behalf. They do all kinds of things for you. As Psalm 103:20–22 states:

PSALM 103:20–22
20 Bless the Lord, ye his angels, that excel in strength, that do his command-ments, hearkening unto the voice of his word.
21 Bless ye the Lord, all ye his hosts; ye ministers of his, that do his pleasure.
22 Bless the Lord, all his works in all places of his dominion: bless the Lord, O my soul.

References to God's hosts and ministers are references to the angelic hosts. God's dominion is where you and I give Him dominion, because He originally gave dominion in the earth to mankind, and He isn't going to take that dominion back. When we take dominion in faith, fighting the good fight of faith, all of this comes to pass on our behalf.

Another reference in Hebrews says this concerning godly angels:

HEBREWS 1:14
14 Are they not all ministering spirits, sent forth to minister for them who shall be heirs of salvation?

Who are the heirs of salvation? Believers are! And the angels are sent forth by God in obedience to the Word that you live and speak. They minister *for* you, not just *to* you. Stated that way, it has a wider implication.

2

Accompanied by Angels

In Second Kings chapter 6, we see where Elisha the prophet of God was in the little town of Dothan when the king of Syria sent his army to capture him. Elisha was there going about God's business. He was there doing what God had sent him to do, although the scripture is not clear on what that was.

Elisha might have been there to minister to an individual, or he might have been there to minister to the whole town. But he was definitely going about the Lord's business in that place, because Elisha was a man who was submitted to God and His purpose in his life.

It had been reported to the king of Syria that the prophet was in Dothan. The king sent his army to capture Elisha and get him out of the way so he could capture the king of Israel.

"Therefore sent he thither horses, and chariots, and a great host" (2 Kings 6:14). What kind of horses and chariots did the king of Syria send against Israel? Natural chariots made with men's hands and natural horses. The passage continues:

What the Servant Saw

2 KINGS 6:14–15

14 and they came by night, and compassed the city about.

15 And when the servant of the man of God was risen early, and gone forth, behold, an host compassed the city both with horses and chariots. And his servant said unto him, Alas, my master! how shall we do?

The prophet's servant looked out, saw the whole place was surrounded by the army of Syria, and said, "What are we going to do? How are we going to escape from this?" It would be frightening to look out and see a whole army surrounding the little town you're in, and you didn't have an army to defend yourself.

What the Prophet Saw

Listen to Elisha's reply in verse 16:

2 KINGS 6:16
16 And he answered, Fear not for they that be with us are more than they that be with them.

Someone was with Elisha, and he knew it. He didn't ask God to show him who was with him; he already knew. It was the angels of God! We need to know this like Elisha knew it.

There is no question about it: Wherever I go—wherever God sends me—I don't go alone. The angels of God go with me. They're with me right now, and they're with you in your room right now, too. When your way is God's way, they're with you wherever you go and whatever you do.

There were other spiritual beings—ungodly beings—present that day, but the ones who were with Elisha were more numerous and powerful than those who came against him. He wasn't really concerned with the natural army. He knew the battle was the Lord's in the spiritual world. That's where battles are won. Furthermore, Elisha knew he was already the victor. He said it when he stated, "There are more with us than those that are with them."

2 KINGS 6:17
17 And Elisha prayed, and said, Lord, I pray thee, open his eyes, that he may see.

Elisha's servant was a young man. He didn't have that developed faith Elisha had.

The Angelic Host

2 KINGS 6:17
17 And the Lord opened the eyes of the young man; and he saw: and, behold, the mountain was full of horses and chariots of fire round about Elisha.

Surrounding Elisha was an angelic host that went with him wherever he went. The angels were there to help him with whatever he needed. He knew it, and he drew upon their presence. They delivered him out of that situation.

Elisha did not stumble into an angels' convention that day. The angels accompanied him to that town, just as they go with you wherever you go for God.

When, like Elisha, you come to a place where the enemy has worked overtime to set a snare and a trap for you, angels are there with you, and they will deliver you. This is what the Word promises, so partake of it. It is just as much a promise of God as the fact that you will be saved if you call on Jesus. It is part of your inheritance.

RULING OVER ALL

Let us now refer to verses 19 and 20 of Psalm 103:

PSALM 103:19–20
19 The Lord hath prepared his throne in the heavens; *and his kingdom ruleth over all.*
20 Bless the Lord, ye his angels, that excel in strength. that do his commandments, hearkening unto the voice of his word.

We have something to thank God for, don't we? In fact, we have more to thank Him for than we can imagine.

Although God's kingdom is ruling over all, it doesn't mean God directs everything that happens in all the kingdoms of the world. Things happen in the kingdoms of the world that are contrary to the will of God. One of the reasons you need the assistance of angels is so you can overcome actions contrary to the will of God that are being performed around you in this world.

In the sense that you believe and act on God's Word, God's kingdom rules over everything contrary to His Word on your behalf.

GOD KEEPS HIS COVENANT PROMISE TO ISRAEL

Sennacherib, the greatest of all the Assyrian kings—the king who had defeated every other nation around him—came to the little nation of Judah and told King Hezekiah and the prophet Isaiah, "Your God can't save you! We're going to take your nation away from you, and you can't stop us. And your God can't keep it from happening." (See Second Chronicles 32.) The king of Assyria blasphemed the God of Israel, didn't he, because God had said He would protect and keep His own covenant people.

If anyone stood in the way of that promise and said, "God can't do it," guess who had to move? It wasn't God, and it wasn't His covenant people. The person who said it couldn't happen—in this case Sennacherib—was the one who had to move.

LEARNING THE HARD WAY

Sennacherib found out the hard way that when you stand in front of God and say, "You can't keep your word for your covenant people," you are going to learn a hard lesson. He and his whole army learned a hard lesson.

It was not God's purpose to destroy Assyrians, but He did what He had to do to deliver Judah in order to keep His word to His covenant people. He did what was necessary.

That night He sent an angel to the camp of the Assyrians, and the angel smote 185,000 soldiers, because they were going to take God's covenant people away in bondage—and His covenant people were believing that God would deliver them!

When you believe God's Word, it will come to pass!

Bear in mind, it is not the desire of God to kill people indiscriminately. Of course not! But if someone stands in the way of what God wants accomplished—if someone attacks you personally, for example, and you stand on your covenant place in the Lord—that person will have to give in, or God may have to remove him in order that you are protected. But you *will* be protected. God will keep His Word to you!

WHEN ANGELS INTERVENE

So even in the natural realm, angels sometimes change circumstances on your behalf when someone tries to stand between you and God's covenant promise to you.

HEBREWS 1:14
14 Are they not all *ministering spirits*, sent forth to minister for them who shall be heirs of salvation?

This verse is a summary of what angels are doing for you today. We will study different aspects of the subject in this first chapter, starting with verse 6:

HEBREWS 1:6
6 And again, when he bringeth in the first begotten into the world, he saith, *And let all the angels of God worship him.*

This speaks of the birth of Jesus in the manger at Bethlehem. Never before had God told His angels to worship another man, had He? And they will never worship any human being other than the man Christ Jesus.

The reason they were commanded to do so is because they would have had an innate reluctance to do so if God had *not* commanded it.

WORSHIPPING GOD IN HUMAN FORM

The angels had always worshipped only God, but now they had to understand that *this was God in human form*. No doubt it was amazing to them and something they couldn't fully understand, because they had never been lost and redeemed.

We understand it, though, don't we? The one thing we human beings understand better than the angels is redemption. We understand what it is like to be lost—separated from God—and then to be redeemed from that fallen state through the blood of Jesus Christ, God's only begotten Son.

Continuing in verse 7:

HEBREWS 1:7

7   And of the angels he saith, Who maketh his angels spirits, and his ministers a flame of fire.

The word for "angels" here is *angelos*, and the word for "ministers" is *liturgos*. Both of these words can apply to human beings, because "angel" literally means "messenger," and *liturgos* means "minister." In this context, the writer is referring to angelic beings.

Remember what Elisha's servant saw around Elisha? Horses and chariots of *fire*. That was the angelic host expressed in a symbolic way.

HEBREWS 1:13–14

13   But to which of the angels said he at any time, Sit on my right hand, until I make thine enemies thy footstool?

14   Are they not all ministering spirits, sent forth to minister for them who shall be heirs of salvation?

SPIRIT BEINGS

The angels are all what? *Ministering spirits.* This means they don't have flesh and blood, and they are not limited by flesh and blood like we are. They can appear as a human being, however, and we will see examples of this as we look further into the Word.

Although angels don't become human beings, they often appear that way to people. It is at the direction of God when they appear that way.

Angels are ministering spirits. They are spirit beings. They have great strength in the spirit world. As we read in Psalm 103:20, angels excel in strength. They far surpass us in strength, because they are not limited by flesh and blood. They are not limited in any human way like we are. Neither are they limited by time and space like we are.

Angels can be limited in what they do, however. If you don't believe, and if you walk in disobedience to God, they can't do what they want to do for you.

CELESTIAL BODIES

Have they any body at all? Angels have what I suppose one could call a *celestial* body. We have a *terrestrial* body of this earth. It's earthy. They have a heavenly body that is not of the same substance, and it does not limit them in any way.

One of these days you are going to have the same kind of a celestial body they have, and it will not be limited in any way like the terrestrial body you now have.

Because we live in a limited flesh-and-blood body today, we need what angels can do for us. They do for us what we cannot do for ourselves. They are *ministering spirits* sent forth to minister for them who shall be heirs of salvation, the writer of Hebrews said in verse 14.

Who are the heirs of salvation? We are! Every born again child of God is an heir of salvation and a joint-heir with Jesus Christ.

WORKING FOR FUTURE HEIRS

Notice the phrase "them who *shall* be heirs of salvation." The angels' work on your behalf certainly doesn't stop when you become an heir of salvation. However, they even worked on your behalf *before* you become an heir of salvation.

They minister for those whose names are written in the Lamb's Book of Life. By God's foreknowledge, He has written your name in that Book of Life. So angels ministered for you even before you were saved. And you probably didn't even know it!

I am grateful for the ministry of angels. Angels saved my life on more than one occasion before I was saved. I wouldn't have lived to get saved if they hadn't done so.

Think about the ugly alternative! If I had died before I was saved, where would I be now? I wouldn't be standing in front of a congregation of shining faces, teaching, that's for sure.

ACTIVATING ANGELIC HELP

If we speak the Word of God, angels hearken to it. If we live according to the Word of God, they hearken to it. If we show forth the glory of God in our life, they are fully empowered to minister for us.

The more we walk in the anointing of God—in other words, the more we walk in obedience to God—the more angels can do for us. Angels can do all kinds of things for us that we cannot do for ourselves. We will examine these as we look at the Word concerning angels.

Remember, *the Word of God is always our authority concerning angels and their ministry.* Their ministry is always centered on the Word. It always agrees with the Word of God and never disagrees with it. It never seems weird. I have to state that, because people often see things and think, "Oh, that's God," but it's not God at all!

If seeming angelic ministry doesn't agree with the Word of God, if it isn't centered in the middle of it, if you can't tell plainly that it's an angelic being working on behalf of God and keeping His commandments, forget it, because angels follow His commandments. They don't follow anyone else's—man's or devil's. Angels keep God's commandments.

AN ANGELIC HITCHHIKER?

When I was teaching about angels and demons in 1982, I came across an interesting story in the November 20, 1982 edition of the monthly *Evangelical Press News*.

I thought it was a tremendous example of how we are instructed that angels don't do anything that doesn't agree with the Word of God. This knowledge will deliver you from a lot of flakiness.

The story relates, "A woman who claims that the hitchhiker she picked up was the Archangel Gabriel is sticking to her story. According to a report from the German Information Center, this housewife from Rosenheim, a town in Bavaria, says she's willing to undergo psychological testing to prove that the sighting was not a figment of her imagination."

I don't think it was. I think she saw what she saw. I think some being appeared to her and did what she said it did—but it wasn't the angel Gabriel.

Two incidents like this happened in Arkansas since that report, and I heard of another incident that happened later in Oklahoma. Someone picked up a hitchhiker who claimed he was Gabriel when he got into the car. He told the driver some things, and then what happened to the German woman happened to the Arkansas and Oklahoma drivers, too.

FALSE PROPHECIES

The German woman reported that she was driving along the Salzburg-Munich Autobahn when she saw what appeared to be an ordinary human hitchhiker and picked him up. He identified himself as the Archangel Gabriel, warned her that the end of the world was imminent, and disappeared into thin air!

Why do we know it wasn't Gabriel? Because he told her that the end of the world was coming in 1984, and everyone knows *it never happened.*

Do angels of God go around giving people false prophecies? Of course not, and people shouldn't go around prophesying falsely, either!

Sometimes this happens, however. Many Christians become overly fascinated with future events. They wonder, "When is everything going to happen?" God isn't the slightest bit interested in such dates, and He doesn't think it is important that you know about those dates. If dates of future happenings were important, the Bible would be full of them.

BEWARE OF PREDICTIONS

But dates are not important, and predicting that a certain event is going to happen on such-and-such a date should not be a part of any legitimate ministry.

In June 1994, someone predicted that all evil was going to be taken out of the world. Look around: Has evil vanished? Someone else said that the end of the world would occur and Jesus would return in September 1994. Now this person is predicting it every year. Sooner of later one of the dates is going to be right, but it won't be to his credit or glory.

Everyone who has ever predicted dates has always been wrong—always, without fail.

Why should we want to join that crowd? God has no interest in predicting dates, and it is not His will to tell us exactly *when* any event is going to happen. The future event itself is what God wants you to know about and be fully persuaded of. When it comes to pass, you will be expecting it if you know what the Word says.

So this being, supposedly the Archangel Gabriel, warned the German woman that the end of the world was imminent and then vanished into thin air. Psychiatrists were called in to verify this vision. I don't suppose they had much success.

NO MAN OR ANGEL KNOWS

Why do we know the vision wasn't genuine? Matthew 24:36 says that *angels know neither the day nor the hour of Jesus' return.* There are two similar references in Mark 13:21 and in Acts 1:7 that state the same thing quite plainly. And what God says plainly, He means plainly.

Jesus declared in Matthew 24:35–36:

MATTHEW 24:35–36
35 Heaven and earth shall pass away, but my words shall not pass away.
36 *But of that day and hour knoweth no man, no, not the angels of heaven, but my Father only.*

Jesus said this right after He told of the general time of His coming in a parable. He has told us that much. He has told us which generation will witness the Second Coming. He has told us what would be happening when it occurs, and He has given us other signs, including the fact that the Gospel first had to be preached throughout the whole world.

But He added, *"of that day and hour knoweth no man, no, not the angels of heaven, but my Father only."* In other words, *the specific time* of either His Second Coming or His coming for the Church is not important. These events are related, and if you knew the date for one, you could determine the date for the other. Nevertheless, Jesus said, *"of that day and hour knoweth no man."*

So anyone who tells you he knows the date of the Second Coming isn't telling you the truth—even if he writes a big book and tries to prove it by scripture. No human being knows—*and no angel knows.* They haven't been told. Jesus said that *only* His Father knows that "day and hour."

NOT EVEN JESUS KNEW

I suppose that even Jesus, as He walked on this earth as the Son of man, didn't know. I'm sure He knows now that He is glorified and seated at the right hand of God, restored to the place from which He came. But when He walked this earth as a man, He didn't know, because His Word wouldn't have been true if He had known.

He said, "No *man* knows," and He is the man Christ Jesus, isn't He? So He didn't know. It is true that no one knows when the Second Coming will occur—and notice that angels are included in that statement.

We saw that there are three New Testament references that no one but God knows the date of Christ's return. The Bible says that in the mouth of two or three witnesses let everything be established, so I just gave you three witnesses.

This is the way you will be able to discern the ministry of godly angels. Their actions always agree with the Word of God. They never do anything that does not agree with the Word.

If the German driver had known what the Bible says, she would never have believed for a minute that her hitchhiker was Gabriel.

Who was it? *Some false spirit got in the car* and then disappeared. His actions were repeated in the reports from Arkansas and Oklahoma: A hitchhiker got in the cars, identified himself as the angel Gabriel, said the end of the world was about to happen, and disappeared. Of course, the date given was different every time, and none of the dates were correct. Such incidents may have happened in many other places that I am unaware of.

SIDETRACKED FROM GOD'S PURPOSE

But these reported incidents were actually other demonic spirits appearing, trying to influence people and draw them away from what God's purpose for their lives is.

If such an evil spirit can get you sidetracked into something that isn't essential or even important, and that becomes your main interest, you won't be involved in anything that *is* important.

False doctrine will take you away from your calling and get you involved in other things, like trying to predict everything that is going to happen.

QUESTIONS ABOUT THE FUTURE

Jesus instructed His disciples to wait for the promise of the Father in Acts 1:5–6:

ACTS 1:5–6
5 For John truly baptized with water, but ye shall be baptized with the Holy Ghost not many days hence.
6 When they therefore were come together, they asked of him, saying, Lord, *wilt thou at this time restore again the kingdom to Israel?*

This was natural human curiosity, and people still have it today. That's why predictions of every sort appeal to people. When the book *On Borrowed Time: 88 Reasons Why the Rapture Will Be in 1988* was written, do you know who bought copies of it?

The books were sold in Christian bookstores, and not a lot of heathens go into Christian bookstores. So Christians, by and large, bought the vast majority of those books because of the curiosity of the natural man, the flesh. Curiosity is there, all right, but don't scratch it! Remember what happened to Adam and Eve.

"It Is Not for You To Know"

Let's look at the next verse, Acts 1:7:

ACTS 1:7
7 And he said unto them [very plainly], *It is not for you to know the times or the seasons,* which the Father hath put in his own power.

By this time, Jesus had been resurrected and glorified, and I'm sure He knew the time of His Second Coming. He knew how long it would take for the Age of Grace to expire, but He didn't share this information with His disciples. The reason He didn't is because it was not important.

When people think they know the exact time of Christ's return, they do weird things. When everyone was reading the *88 Reasons* book, many Christians, including some I knew, sold everything they owned in the summer of that year and gave all the proceeds to their churches. Why? Because they had a date for the Second Coming: September 1988.

Noble and Carnal Motives

They had a noble motive, but I wonder what they've been doing since? They didn't think they were going to need their possessions after September 1988.

Others were more carnal than that. They ran up their credit cards to the maximum, because they didn't think they would be around to pay for what they had bought! And they've been paying off all that credit card debt ever since.

One reason God doesn't tell us dates is because it stirs up carnal actions in us. When people think they know when something is going to happen, many go out and do carnal things—and God isn't going to do anything that will stir up carnality in the Church.

ANGELS DON'T PREDICT DATES

We know the hitchhiker wasn't Gabriel. How do we know? By the Word of God. It's plain, isn't it? Some will ask, "Why are you making such a big deal out of this?" Because I've had Bible school students sit in my classroom, hear the same thing I'm teaching you now, and go out after graduation and have an "angelic visitation" that told them when the Lord was going to return—and they started to preach it!

No matter how bright the light is that appears to you, it isn't an angel if he tells you dates for the Lord's return. The angel Gabriel didn't even tell Mary the date she was going to bear the baby Jesus!

I'm sure she could have figured it out, knowing how long it takes to have a baby, but the date of His birth was not the angel's message. He just said, "You are going to bear a son." He told her what to name the child, but he didn't tell her the date of the birth. It wasn't important.

Angels of God do not deliver dates, and we shouldn't, either!

3

SCRIPTURAL FACTS ABOUT ANGELS

Now let's look at a few scriptural facts about angels.

First, God created all the angels. Every angel that was created was created by God.

Also, angels are not a race. They don't reproduce themselves. There are no baby angels. There are different ranks of angels, created in different categories and order of ministry, but there are no baby angels. Many people think there are.

When you see artwork about angelic beings, you frequently see little baby angels, but there are no baby angels floating around Heaven. What good would a baby angel do you, anyway? If they were like human babies, they would not be able to help you much.

So although angels are different in the order of their creation, God created every one of them. John 1:3 says that without Jesus Christ, nothing was made that was made. That seals the matter, doesn't it?

NO OTHER CREATOR

There is no other creator. Satan can't create anything. He tried to, but look where it got him. You and I are not creators. We can be creative in God's creative power by agreeing with God's Word, but we don't create anything. God does. We take dominion in the earth, but He is the Creator. Everything that was ever created, God created, and nothing is ever going to be created by anyone else.

I can save a lot of scientists a lot of time trying to create some new life form from DNA in their laboratories. They are not going to be able to do it. There is no Creator except God. And there never was a real Frankenstein!

Second, every angel was also created holy. As we know from Ezekiel 28, Isaiah 14, and Revelation 12, Satan decided to live otherwise, and he persuaded other angelic beings created by God to follow his example. They ignored God's warnings and became what they are today—fallen angels.

However, two-thirds of the angels did not follow Satan and fall. I am sure Satan was trying to influence all of them, not just one-third, but two-thirds didn't follow him. That's good. It means there are more godly angels than there are fallen angels. The godly angels are still living in the power of God, and the other kind are not.

Third, angels were created to be limited and dependent upon God. There is a limitation in the order of their creation, although that limitation is not the same as ours. It far surpasses ours, but angels are still limited by God's Word to do what they are supposed to do and what God created them to do. For example, they don't just roam around doing whatever they want. They perform the will of God. What God made them for is what you will find them doing.

THE ARCHANGEL MICHAEL'S REBUKE

Angels are totally limited and dependent upon God for everything they do. You can see that from the account in Jude 9 that describes how the Archangel Michael, when he disputed with the devil concerning the body of Moses, did not bring a railing accusation against the devil, but simply said, *"The Lord rebuke thee."* That was pretty simple, wasn't it? That's all it took.

God had a purpose for removing the body of Moses from the earth. Can you imagine what would have become of it if the Jewish nation had been allowed to keep it? They would surely have made a god out of it and worshipped it.

We, too, are beings—human beings—who are limited and dependent on God for everything we do. As we saw in Hebrews 1:14, angels are spirit beings who operate in the spirit realm. They cause things to happen in the natural realm on your behalf, but they are not flesh and blood, and neither are they omnipresent or omniscient. Although they know a lot more than we do, they are not all-knowing. God is the only omniscient One.

Angels know some things far beyond what we know; but, on the other hand, we know some things they don't know. They desire to look into salvation, it says in First Peter 1:12. They desire to understand it. And they are joyful about it, because to them it is the greatest thing that ever happened.

WHEN ANGELS LEAP FOR JOY

A human being walking in darkness—wrapped up in it, deceived and bound by things of darkness—can get set free by believing what Jesus has done. Every time the angels see someone accept the gift of salvation, they leap for joy, because the Word of God is coming to pass.

When I am standing in church watching people get saved, I have to remind myself that the angels are jumping for joy at that moment, and I shouldn't be standing there thinking, "Ho hum, I wonder what time we're going to get to the restaurant?"

People being born again is something to be joyful and excited about! Even if it is just one person, the angels of God jump for joy, because the power of God has been manifested to deliver another human being out of bondage and darkness into His glorious kingdom. At that moment, they see what actually happens a lot more clearly than we do.

Angels that fell lost their holiness, because they left their first estate; in other words, they left that place of being dependent on the Godhead and responsible to the Godhead. They left it to do their own will.

People get into all kinds of unprofitable disputes trying to figure out how many angels there are. In the Middle Ages, scholars argued the burning question: "How many angels can dance on the head of a pin?" Who cares? What has that got to do with anything?

As we saw in Hebrews 12:22, angels are an innumerable company—more than man can imagine or count. Revelation 5:11 says there are hundreds of millions and millions more. Jeremiah 33:22 says that the host of Heaven cannot be numbered. If they can't be numbered, there is no sense trying to number them.

Creation Reflects the Creator

Scripture shows us that all of the creation of God reflects Him. Everything God created shows evidence of Himself. And in the case of spirit beings, there is the image and likeness of God. The entire creation reveals that God exists. Everything He made reflects that fact.

Paul teaches this plainly in the first chapter of Romans. It proves to anyone who is interested that God exists. But you need to know more than the fact that He exists, don't you? If you seek the God you know exists, you will find the truth of the Gospel.

So angelic beings are created in God's image and likeness. They show His image and likeness. They show that, like God, they possess intellect, sensibility, an emotional self, and their own will.

Their intellect is greatly developed, far surpassing ours. They are full of joy when someone repents, and they are grieved when we walk contrary to the will and purpose of God.

Angels Can Exercise Their Will

Although they have an emotional self just like we human beings do, angels are not ruled by it. They are ruled by God's will. That they have their own will is proven by the fact that a third of them chose to follow the devil, but two thirds of them chose not to. *Angels can exercise their will!*

I have heard some teachings about angels in the past that were not true. These teachers said that angelic beings are more or less robots who have been programmed by God, and they can only do what God programmed them to do.

That is not true! Angels do have a will. They were created in the image and likeness of God. They have a power of choice just like we do! However, they have always chosen to glorify and do the will of

God. That is a wonderful thing to behold, and it is a good example for us.

GOD DEALS WITH JOB

In Job chapter 38, God appeared to Job after his friends, the miserable comforters, were finished with him. He started to deal with Job about where he had missed it and gone astray. Job's friends couldn't seem to communicate properly in that area. They tried to fix blame and do all sorts of things God wasn't interested in.

JOB 38:1–3
1 Then the Lord answered Job out of the whirlwind, and said,
2 Who is this that darkeneth counsel by words without knowledge?
3 Gird up now thy loins like a man: for I will demand of thee, and answer thou me.

In other words; God was saying, "Job, if you know as much as you think you do, you ought to be able to answer these questions. Gird up your loins now like a man, and answer me."

JOB 38:4–7
4 Where wast thou when I laid the foundations of the earth? declare, if thou hast understanding.
5 Who hath laid the measures thereof, if thou knowest? or who hath stretched the line upon it?
6 Whereupon are the foundations thereof fastened? or who laid the corner stone thereof;
7 When the morning stars sang together, and all the sons of God shouted for joy?

WHERE WAS JOB?

God asked Job where he was when God laid the foundations of the earth. He asked him if he knew who had put all of creation in balance so it would remain like God had created it.

"Where were you, Job, when things were in that state? Before sin even was, before Lucifer decided to disobey Me, before any of those things happened, were you around, Job?"

Job wasn't in existence yet. Job didn't know as much as he thought he did! That was about to be made clear to him. He was about to repent and say, "I don't know anything. I repent in sackcloth and ashes."

Notice in verse 7 that there was a time when the angelic host rejoiced because of the order of their creation. They shouted for joy! They were full of praise to God. A manifestation of glory came forth from them. Job heard all this from God Himself.

ANGELS IN ACTION

Isaiah chapter 6 shows us how the angels of God perform things when they are in action and what happens.

ISAIAH 6:1–2
1   In the year that king Uzziah died I saw also the Lord sitting upon a throne, high and lifted up, and his train filled the temple.
2   Above it stood the seraphims.

Seraphims are a very high type of angel; high in the order of their creation. God's glory filled the Temple, and above His glory stood these angelic beings, the seraphims.

ISAIAH 6:2–4
2   Each one had six wings; with twain he covered his face, with twain he covered his feet, and with twain he did fly.
3   And one cried unto another, and said, Holy, holy, holy, is the Lord of hosts: the whole earth is full of his glory.
4   And the posts of the door moved at the voice of him that cried, and the house was filled with smoke.

When the angels rejoiced in God's holiness, the whole place was shaken. I would judge from this that angels are very powerful beings! When they praised God, it had a powerful effect on everything around them.

ANGELIC SINGING

I once heard angelic singing. It happened shortly after I received the baptism in the Holy Spirit at Beale Air Force base in California, where I was stationed.

I was new to the Charismatic Movement, but many people in surrounding communities near the base were Charismatics. One day the chaplain asked me if I would like to go with him to a Bible study in one of the little towns nearby.

I went with him and another man, and when we arrived, the people were already worshipping God. We joined in the worship, and it was the most beautiful singing I had ever heard. I thought, "Man, these people can really sing!" We were singing in the Spirit and singing with our understanding, and we sang for about half an hour before the teaching of the Word of God began.

I went home thrilled and transformed by the music, because I was used to organ music that sounded like a funeral march every time I went to church. And I didn't appreciate the people who were trying to out-sing each other in the choir. So I developed a whole new appreciation for worship and for music that night.

A week later when the chaplain asked if I wanted to return, I quickly agreed. We went there and sat in the same room, and we all sang together. But it wasn't like the first time. I thought, "What happened to them? They aren't singing like they did last week. Why don't they sound like they did last week?"

BEYOND THE NATURAL REALM

But the week before, I had heard something that was *beyond the natural realm*! Sometimes when you rejoice or worship, God opens your eyes or your senses to see or hear something that is beyond the natural realm. I had heard music that was beyond the natural realm!

The angelic beings that were present with the saints that night joined in, and I heard them. It was marvelous! It was wonderful! It was beyond my experience that anything could be so beautiful, so exciting to listen to, and so full of life.

That's the way angels are. God made them to worship like that. And that's the way we ought to worship and rejoice. God made us to worship and rejoice just like that. We can even get started in this lifetime.

As someone said, "If you don't like to shout, you'd better change your mind, because in Heaven there's going to be a lot of shouting!" If you don't like things that are loud, you'd better change your mind about that, too, because there will be something louder than you ever heard when you get to Heaven.

When an expression of worship or rejoicing is truly from God, you had better get used to it and start doing it now.

There are other places in scripture where we see angels rejoice. Luke 15:10, for example, tells how angels rejoice when one sinner repents.

Angelic Zeal

Angelic beings are zealous for God and His holiness. They contend for the essence of His character. They do not have to defend God—He doesn't need defense—but they won't agree with anything contrary to Him, and they will disagree with what is contrary to Him. Sometimes that disagreement takes a strong outward form, as it did in the following story from Acts.

ACTS 12:21–23

21 And upon a set day Herod, arrayed in royal apparel, sat upon his throne, and made an oration unto them.

22 And the people gave a shout, saying, It is the voice of a god, and not of a man.

23 And immediately the angel of the Lord smote him, because he gave not God the glory: and he was eaten of worms, and gave up the ghost.

Who was Herod? He was the king of Israel, sitting on the throne of David. Herod was an Edomite, which means he was a descendant of Esau.

Why was he sitting on the throne of Israel? Because the Romans put him there. Why did they put him on the throne of Israel? To slap the Israelites right in the face!

What could possibly have been more degrading to Israel than to have a descendant of Esau ruling over them? Herod and all his ancestors were descendants of the Edomite nation.

So the Romans put Herod on the throne of Israel, but they didn't do this just to Israel; they did it to most nations they conquered. They chose someone those people despised and put him on their throne to humble and humiliate them.

MISPLACED ZEAL

One day Herod gave a speech, and the people shouted, "It is the voice of a god and not a man!" What should Herod's response have been? "No, no, no, no! I'm just a man!"

Do you remember the time when Paul and Barnabas ran into an overly enthusiastic crowd in Iconium who believed they were the gods Jupiter and Mercury come to earth in the flesh?

Horrified, Paul and Barnabas tore their clothing and ran among the people, shouting, "We're just human beings! We're not Jupiter, Mercury, or whomever else you think we are!" That was their immediate response; they didn't allow the error to linger in the minds of the people for a moment. (See Acts 14.)

As the king who sat on the throne of David, Herod knew he should not be confusing himself with God or allowing anyone else to do it, either, when the people cried, *"It is the voice of a god, and not of a man."*

"And immediately the angel of the Lord smote him." This wasn't the action of some *fallen* angel; this was a godly angel.

THE PENALTY FOR STEALING GOD'S GLORY

"The angel of the Lord smote him, because he gave not God the glory: and he was eaten of worms, and gave up the ghost. But the word of God grew and multiplied" (Acts 12:23–24).

Why did God instruct the angel to do that? So the Word of God in its fledgling hour—right at the beginning of the Gospel Age—would not be snuffed out by someone who took God's glory for himself.

That's how zealous angels are. Zeal is an emotional thing. It changes you. It fires you up. It causes you to do something mighty. It calls forth an emotional response that affects the whole person. Angelic beings are like that: They are zealous for God and His kingdom.

4

Getting Along With Angels

The next thing we want to look at is how angelic beings walk with you in agreement when you walk in agreement with God.

If you walk in the flesh and deliberately disobey God, angels cannot walk in agreement with that attitude. In other words, they don't function the same for a person who walks in disobedience as they do for one who walks in obedience.

This explains why certain things happen. For example, accidents sometimes befall good Christian people. Why didn't the angels do something about those situations? We don't know exactly why, but why do the angels intervene in other cases?

There is a difference in what *we* do, not in what *they* do. They will make the same response every time; they will always respond the same way to certain situations. God is not a respecter of persons (Acts 10:34), and He does not act erratically.

What we do makes the difference. In many cases, the closeness of our walk with God determines whether the angels can act on our behalf or not.

Amos 3:3 asks, *"Can two walk together, except they be agreed?"* We must be in agreement with what we know of God for the angels to walk with us, because they will not walk in agreement with the flesh, with disobedience, or with anything else contrary to the will of God.

"Be Ye Not Unequally Yoked Together"

In Second Corinthians 6:14, Paul wrote concerning unbelievers: *"Be ye not unequally yoked together with unbelievers."* Do *not* be yoked together with unbelievers! The passage continues:

2 CORINTHIANS 6:14–18

14 For what fellowship hath righteousness with unrighteousness? and what communion hath light with darkness?

15 And what concord [or agreement] hath Christ with Belial [the devil]? or what part hath he that believeth with an infidel?

16 And what agreement hath the temple of God with idols? for ye are the temple of the living God; as God hath said, I will dwell in them, and walk in them, and I will be their God, and they shall be my people.

17 Wherefore come out from among them, and be ye separate [you be separate from the world's ways], saith the Lord, and touch not the unclean thing; and I will receive you.

18 And will be a Father unto you, and ye shall be my sons and daughters, saith the Lord Almighty.

When Angels Are Absent

This is not only God's direction to us; it is also the angels' direction from God (His commandment), and they keep it perfectly. They don't wander in and out of disobedience like many human beings do. So if they are not present at some point in a human being's life to deliver him or her, it is not because the angels missed it; it is because the human being did.

I don't intend for this to be a legalistic principle, however. God is not waiting for you to make one little misstep so He can swat you down. That's not the way He is. God always gives us space to repent— always, always, always!

He commands angels to do His commandments, and whatever He will do, they will obey. Let's look at a few scriptures that bear this out.

One of these passages is found in the Book of Exodus, where it speaks of the angel of the Lord that would lead Israel into their inheritance. In Exodus 23:20–21, God said:

EXODUS 23:20–21

20 Behold, I send an Angel before thee, to keep thee in the way, and to bring thee into the place which I have prepared.

21 Beware of him, and obey his voice, provoke him not.

Provoking Angels

Notice *it is possible for us to provoke an angel!* Don't provoke him by living in the flesh according to the lusts of the flesh. Don't provoke him by disobeying God.

Verse 21 continues: *"For he will not pardon your transgressions."*

The angel cannot do this. He isn't God. *"For my name is in him."*

God's holiness, God's righteousness, and God's just character are in him.

EXODUS 23:22–23

22 But if thou shalt indeed obey his voice, and do all that I speak; then I will be an enemy unto thine enemies, and an adversary unto thine adversaries.

23 For mine Angel shall go before thee, and bring thee in unto [this land that was promised to you].

The angel is there to minister for you, yet you can provoke him. It *is* possible. You should not want to do that, should you? This means you should think seriously about things before acting on them or speaking about them.

THE MARRIAGE RELATIONSHIP

Another indication of this is found in First Corinthians chapter 11. This is a little more complicated and more difficult to apply, but the principle is here in the New Testament nonetheless.

In this chapter, Paul is discussing men and women in families; in other words, husbands and wives in the marriage relationship, not *all* men and all women. Some people miss this point entirely.

Verses 7 through 10 read:

1 CORINTHIANS 11:7–10

7 For a man indeed ought not to cover his head, for as much as he is the image and glory of God: but the woman is the glory of the man.

8 For the man is not of the woman; but the woman of the man.

9 Neither was the man created for the woman; but the woman for the man.

10 For this cause ought the woman to have power on her head because of the angels.

A SIGN OF AUTHORITY

The word "power" there is *exousia* in Greek. It means "authority." So a head covering is really a sign of *authority* on the woman's head.

Before we go any further, I want to note that in our day we do not have any such custom in the majority of the Church.

What was the sign of authority that the woman wore on her head? *It was submission to her husband.* Does the Word of God require that today? Yes, it does, but not in the same physical manifestation that existed nearly 2000 years ago. A sign of submission to those women was different from what it is to women today.

Modern women don't necessarily show their submission to their husbands by what they put on their heads. They may not put anything on their heads; in fact, most women today don't.

I remember in the beginning of the Charismatic Movement in the early '60s, I went to a meeting in Sacramento, California. There had been good teaching previously in that particular church, but, all of a sudden, they held a big meeting and brought a guest speaker to an auditorium.

When the women from that church came into the auditorium, they were all wearing little coverings on their heads.

It looked like they had taken the doilies off their end tables and put them on their heads! I'm serious. I think that's what most of them did!

They had read this passage of scripture and decided, "We've got to keep our heads covered to be in submission to our husbands." There are a lot of other ways a woman can show submission without having something on her head. And, remember, we don't have any such custom in most churches today.

A DILEMMA OF CONSCIENCE

A few years ago, a young woman from a Mennonite background came to the Bible school where I teach, and she wore a covering on her head, because the Mennonites continue that custom.

After she had been at school for several months, she realized there wasn't another woman in school wearing anything like her little bonnet, so she came to me for advice.

She asked, "Should I continue to wear this?"

I replied, "Don't ask me. You're asking the wrong person. Ask your own conscience. Let your conscience guide you."

She said, "All right, I will." Then she told me she wore the head covering out of respect for her family. She didn't want to offend them by not wearing it.

I thought, "If you keep wearing it, that's a good reason." And she did continue to wear it. She wore it throughout the whole first year. By the time second year arrived, she was no longer wearing it.

She had realized that wearing it had become unnecessary for her. She had realized that a woman can show submission and respect to her husband and parents in other ways; it isn't proven simply by what she puts on her head. On the other hand, she didn't want to make anyone stumble, either.

In certain parts of the world, we find people who maintain a custom like that today—in the whole Arab world, for example. When we make headway in the Arab world and start preaching the Gospel, the first thing we *don't* want to tell the women is, "Take the covering off your head. Get rid of your veil."

WHAT IS IMPORTANT

Doing so would incite trouble with their husbands, families, neighbors, and the general public, because the custom is so entrenched. What is important is not whether a woman has something on her head or not; showing respect to another person is what counts.

"For this cause ought the woman to have power [a sign of authority] *on her head."* What is the sign of authority that the angels notice and heed? *Submission to God,* because that is being obedient to God's Word.

There are many other ways women can show submission to their husbands, and angels watch to see if you are doing that, ladies. But men aren't let off the hook here. Angels watch to see how well you love your wives, gentlemen, because that is also a sign of obedience to God.

So it is not just women God is concerned about; He is concerned about the whole Body of Christ—men and women alike. We all have commandments we are under and need to keep.

WHAT ANGELS LOOK FOR

Our submission to God is what the angels are looking for. And when you are in submission as a wife to your husband, you are in submission to God. That is God's commandment to you. Wives should not feel bad about that. It is what God has required.

On the other hand, God has required a husband to show the love of Christ to his wife and to love her as he loves his own body. God says when men do that, it shows submission to Him.

We read in First Corinthians chapter 11 that *"For this cause ought the woman to have power on her head because of the angels"* (v. 10). The woman in this case shows her authority or a sign of authority to the angelic beings. The angelic beings are looking for your obedience in following God's order in God's way.

Did you know that one of the things angels are called in scripture is "watchers"? They are watching you. Again, not legalistically, and not so they can punish you at the first sign of a mistake. That's not their function at all. But they are watching you, your lifestyle, and what you say. They are observing you. We will see later that they watch other people as well.

THE JUDGMENT OF GODLY ANGELS

People need to be careful how they treat the things of God. Often, unbelievers find themselves under the judgment executed by godly angels if they try to keep others from having what God says is theirs.

For example, a civil authority who says you can't preach the Gospel doesn't have any authority to say that. Judging spiritual or church matters is not part of the authority that is invested in him. He is clearly going beyond his authority if he interferes.

Peter and John had that experience when the religious leaders of the day—who were also the civil leaders of that day in Israel—commanded the disciples to no longer preach the Gospel (Acts 4:18).

Peter and John responded, "Whether or not we preach the Gospel and what becomes of us because we do, you may decide. But as for us, we can only preach because God commanded us to. And we cannot obey the commandment of a man when we have a commandment of God."

Notice they didn't rail or get mad at the leaders. They made their statement respectfully and even said, "You may decide what becomes of us when we preach, because you have authority to do so."

If someone tries to keep you from doing what God has commanded you to do or keep you from being blessed the way God says He is going to bless you, something is going to have to give—and it will not be you if your attitude is right.

THE KING'S MISTAKE

We saw that in the last chapter in the case of Sennacherib, king of Assyria. He surrounded Jerusalem, the southern kingdom, with his army and was about to burn the city and take all the people captive, as he had done to many other nations.

He taunted King Hezekiah and all the people who were listening on the city wall, saying that God would not be able to deliver them as He had promised. He threatened the Jews with famine and thirst, attempting to terrorize them into surrendering.

Sennacherib and his servants spoke many disparaging things against God. He even wrote letters, according to Second Chronicles 32:17!

2 CHRONICLES 32:17

17 To rail on the Lord God of Israel, and to speak against him, saying, As the gods of the nations of other lands have not delivered their people out of my hand, so shall not the God of Hezekiah deliver his people out of mine hand.

Sennacherib did not realize that God had *not* told the Jews, "I can deliver you from the sword and the famine—except when Sennacherib comes." What God had actually promised was that He could deliver His own people from sword and famine, and He said He would if they would call upon Him. That was His word and His covenant with them.

King Hezekiah and the prophet Isaiah prayed and cried to heaven.

"And the Lord Sent an Angel"

2 CHRONICLES 32:21–22

21 And the Lord sent an angel, which cut off all the mighty men of valour and the leaders and captains in the camp of the king of Assyria. So he [the king] returned home with shame of face to his own land. And when he was come into the house of his god, they that came forth of his own bowels [his sons] slew him there with the sword.

22 Thus the Lord saved Hezekiah and the inhabitants of Jerusalem from the hand of Sennacherib the king of Assyria.

If you read history, you will find that King Sennacherib was the king of his day; the most powerful king on earth. When he said he had defeated all those other nations, he was not speaking idly. He had defeated them all. Not one had ever defeated him before he came to the little nation of Judah. It didn't look like the Jews could defend themselves, either.

King Sennacherib didn't understand the covenant, and he didn't understand a covenant-keeping God—THE God—not some god made with hands and empowered with a demon.

God kept His word to Israel by sending the angel of the Lord to slay 185,000 Assyrians. God does not take any pleasure in the death of the wicked, the Bible says (Ezekiel 18:23, 32; 33:11), and we shouldn't take any pleasure when our enemies are destroyed, either. We ought to be grieved.

The Lord was grieved that this had to happen, but He saw to it that His covenant was kept. If He had not thoroughly defeated the king of Assyria at that time, Sennacherib would have promptly returned in another attempt to destroy the Jews.

PRESENT BUT INVISIBLE

Another thing about angels is that normally they are invisible to your senses, even though they are present with you all the time, the Bible tells us, when you are walking in obedience to God.

You don't see angels all the time, but you *can* see them when God allows it. So although it is possible for you to see angels, it is rare if you do. It is normal *not* to see them. However, angels are always with you, whether you see them or not.

Another example we saw earlier was in Second Kings 6:17, where Elisha the prophet prayed for his servant's eyes to be opened to see the fiery horses and chariots surrounding them.

Elisha knew they were there to protect him. He knew God had promised in Psalm 91 that the angels of God would protect him. He understood by his covenant with God what was his to have and appropriate by faith.

But Elisha asked for his young servant, who hadn't developed that kind of faith, to see the angelic host. The young man saw them with his natural eyes—but they were there all the time. They were there before he saw them, and they were there afterwards.

DON'T SEEK FOR VISIONS OF ANGELS

Angels can, at the direction of God, appear to human beings in the sensory realm, where you actually see them. They can appear in all their glory, or they can appear like a human being, but that is always at the direction of God. And asking to see angels is not an experience we should seek!

I knew a Christian man—a pastor—who sought to see angels. And he did, all right. The book he wrote tells what kind of angels he saw. The whole thing was totally beyond the Word of God. Angels do not bring revelation beyond the Word of God. Their revelation is always totally in agreement with it.

In the first chapter of Luke, we find that an angel appeared to Zacharias the priest while he was offering incense in the Temple. The Bible simply says that Zacharias was doing his job at the Temple. He wasn't in the Temple seeking to see an angel. He wasn't praying, "O God, send me an angel. I want to see an angel!"

Kenneth Copeland said that years ago he heard both Kenneth E. Hagin and Oral Roberts tell of visions God had granted them. Because he was beginning in the ministry, Brother Copeland prayed, "Lord, I need to have a vision like Brother Hagin and Oral Roberts had."

He recalled, "God didn't even answer me." So he asked God two or three more times, and God finally said, "Kenneth, I'll give you a vision, but if I do, it will set your ministry back five years."

Brother Copeland replied, "Okay. I don't need a vision!"

WALK BY FAITH, NOT BY SIGHT

It is not God's will for you to go around seeking for a vision, and you don't need one anyway. *You are doing the will of God just by walking by faith!* He doesn't want you to walk by sight.

By this, I do not mean that all visions are based on unbelief. No, most visions come to people when it is necessary for them to know something. Why are these visions necessary? Probably there isn't anyone around who can tell the person that information or truth.

An example is when the risen Christ appeared to Paul during the three years when He taught him in the desert. There was no one on earth qualified to teach Paul what Jesus Christ told him. The visions of Kenneth E. Hagin, Oral Roberts, and others occurred in much the same circumstances. So angels can appear, but when they do, it is always at the direction of God.

GABRIEL'S MESSAGES

Returning to Zacharias' story in Luke 1:

LUKE 1:8–11

8   And it came to pass, that while he [Zacharias] executed the priest's office before God in the order of his course,

9 According to the custom of the priest's office, his lot was to burn incense when he went into the temple of the Lord.

10 And the whole multitude of the people were praying without at the time of incense.

11 And there appeared unto him an angel of the Lord standing on the right side of the altar of incense.

The priest Zacharias saw Gabriel. With his own eyes, he saw him standing there! God had sent the angel to give Zacharias the message that he and his wife, Elisabeth, would have a child, who was to be named John. This child would grow up to be John the Baptist.

Gabriel also did something to keep Zacharias from saying anything that would hinder the promise from coming to pass: Zacharias was struck speechless until the baby's birth!

AT GOD'S DIRECTION

Then Gabriel was sent by God, it says in verse 26, in the sixth month to Mary. Notice angels are always sent by God. When God directs an angel to appear to you, it is always at His direction. It is not at man's direction, nor is your own carnal request being answered.

LUKE 1:26–27

26 And in the sixth month the angel Gabriel was sent from God unto a city of Galilee, named Nazareth.

27 To a virgin espoused to a man whose name was Joseph, of the house of David: and the virgin's name was Mary.

Gabriel told Mary what would befall her, she believed him, and it all happened.

DREAMS AND VISIONS

In Daniel chapter 8, the angel Gabriel literally appeared to Daniel in a vision in response to his prayers of supplication for himself and the exiled nation of Israel. In this instance, the angel communicated revelations to Daniel about things he needed to know.

Angels can appear in both dreams and visions. Angels appeared to Daniel, Jacob, and many other people at various times in visions and dreams. There is not much difference between visions and dreams, other than the fact that in one of them you are awake and in the other you are asleep.

You will find in Matthew chapter 1 that Joseph, who was to be the husband of Mary and the earthly father of Jesus, had visions and dreams where angels appeared to him, as we see from this passage:

MATTHEW 1:19–21, 24

19 Then Joseph her husband, being a just man, and not willing to make her a public example, was minded to put her away privily.

20 But while he thought on these things, behold, the angel of the Lord appeared unto him in a dream, saying, Joseph, thou son of David, fear not to take unto thee Mary thy wife: for that which is conceived in her is of the Holy Ghost.

21 And she shall bring forth a son, and thou shalt call his name JESUS: for he shall save his people from their sins.

24 Then Joseph being raised from sleep did as the angel of the Lord had bidden him, and took unto him his wife.

TRUSTING GOD

Those were astounding things that Joseph and Mary heard from the angels that spoke to them! They had to have been prepared spiritually to receive such visitations. In other words, they weren't just starting to learn how to believe God the day the angels appeared to them; they already had knowledge of God and His ways.

When you and I were just starting out in the Christian walk, if some angel had appeared to us and told us things like that, we wouldn't have known how to handle it.

Joseph didn't understand what he was told in the dream, but he believed it, because it was sent from God, and he recognized it was sent from God. He didn't understand the message anymore than you do.

Do you understand the virgin birth? Can you explain it biologically? I can't either, but I believe it, don't you? Do you believe there was a virgin birth? Absolutely!

UNQUESTIONING FAITH

Angels appeared to Joseph several times in dreams, warning him of danger to the child Jesus (see Matthew 2). Joseph immediately obeyed these warnings. He didn't consult with other people, asking, "Do you think this warning is from God?"

He knew the warnings were from God. He knew there was a Messiah coming. He believed it. And when God told him through an angel that the Messiah would come into Joseph's own family, he didn't question it.

God can do all things. With God all things are possible, but we don't know *how* He does everything. Many people get hung up on such questions as: "How is God going to do this?" "How is He going to do that?" "How is He going to get me out of this predicament?"

These are questions you should never be concerned about, because they are based in unbelief. Just think about what God said He would do, and be assured He knows how to do it.

THERE ARE NO FEMALE ANGELS

Throughout both the Old and New Testaments, we find many instances where angels appeared to people.

When angels appear, they appear in the form of men. That's not because God is a chauvinist, ladies, but *angels do not appear in the female form in the Bible.*

I realize artists have depicted them as women, and I have seen cute little bedtime stories written about female angels, but the Bible does not depict angels that way.

Again, God is not prejudiced against women, but I believe this is something He has done so we can identify what is of God and what is not of God.

GEORGE WASHINGTON'S VISION

George Washington reportedly had a vision where a woman with wings appeared to him and revealed the future of the United States. I know many of you have read this vision.

Washington was a fine man. We call him the father of our country. At the time of the Revolutionary War, God helped him mightily to overcome the tremendous odds that were stacked against him and this nation.

But Washington is not the source of all truth; the Word of God is. I don't care *who* they are—if people's experiences do not measure up with the Word of God, we should disregard their experiences. We will see more about this later.

ENTERTAINING ANGELS UNAWARES

HEBREWS 13:1–2

1 Let brotherly love continue.
2 Be not forgetful to entertain strangers: for thereby some have entertained angels unawares.

Some have entertained angels unawares! If a host thinks he is entertaining another human being, but it is actually an angel, that angelic being looked exactly like a human, acted like one, and even partook of food and drink.

There are two ways people entertain angels unawares. First, an angel appears to you, and thus you "entertain" him. Or, second, when you entertain another believer, holy angels you aren't aware of are present. Although you could entertain angels either way, I am convinced their appearance happens both ways.

ABRAHAM'S HOSPITALITY

In Genesis chapter 18, something like that happened in an angelic appearance to Abraham. The angel of the Lord—the Lord Himself—appeared on earth as an angel, accompanied by two angels. *All three appeared as normal human beings.*

I'm sure that when Abraham first saw them, he didn't know who they were; but as things progressed, he began to realize who had come to visit him. The story begins:

GENESIS 18:1–4

1 And the Lord appeared unto him in the plains of Mamre: and he sat in the tent door in the heat of the day;

2 And he lift up his eyes and looked, and, lo, three men stood by him, and when he saw them, he ran to meet them from the tent door, and bowed himself toward the ground,

3 And said, My Lord, if now I have found favour in thy sight, pass not away, I pray thee, from thy servant:

4 Let a little water, I pray you, be fetched, and wash your feet, and rest yourselves under the tree.

ABRAHAM SEES THE LORD

Three normal-appearing men stood near Abraham's tent, and Abraham hastened to perform the normal hospitality he would show to any person who came along to his encampment in the heat of the day. The way he addressed the first angel was normal hospitality as well.

Abraham served these angels unawares. He had food prepared for them and fed them. Finally he began to realize he was talking to the Lord!

The Lord appeared as a normal man here. Do you think if God appeared to you in all His glory, you would be interested in washing His feet? You would be so awestruck, you wouldn't even be thinking about whether He had dust on His feet or not. The Lord conversed with Abraham and Sarah about the coming of Isaac.

The story continues:

GENESIS 18:16–18, 20–22

16 And the men rose up from thence, and looked toward Sodom: and Abraham went with them to bring them on the way.

17 And the Lord said, Shall I hide from Abraham that thing which I do;

18 Seeing that Abraham shall surely become a great and mighty nation, and all the nations of the earth shall be blessed in him?

20 And the Lord said, Because the cry of Sodom and Gomorrah is great, and because their sin is very grievous;

21 I will go down now, and see whether they have done altogether according to the cry of it, which is come unto me; and if not, I will know.

22 And the men turned their faces from thence, and went toward Sodom: but Abraham stood yet before the Lord.

Abraham Intercedes for Sodom

So the two angels who appeared as men turned their faces toward Sodom, but the angel of the Lord stayed with Abraham. And Abraham, as we know, then made intercession for that place, bargaining with the Lord over sparing the immoral city if a certain number of righteous persons could be found in it.

The Lord kept answering him, "Yes, Abraham, I'll spare it for that many. Yes, Abraham, I'll spare it for that many." Finally Abraham bargained to the point of asking, "If there were *ten* righteous men there, would You spare Sodom?"

The Lord answered, "Yes, I will." But evidently there weren't ten righteous men in the whole city!

What else did Abraham do? He interceded for his nephew Lot and his family, who lived in the wicked city of Sodom. The text doesn't say Abraham did this, but I know he did, because the Word says, *"God remembered Abraham* [his intercession], *and sent Lot out of the midst of the over throw, when he overthrew the cities in the which Lot dwelt"* (Gen. 19:29).

Lot Reluctantly Leaves Sodom

Lot left Sodom before the city was destroyed. The two angels escorted his family and him out. Lot wasn't particularly anxious to leave, and the angels almost had to drag him out, but they finally succeeded in getting him to leave before it was too late.

I'm sure the successful escape of Lot and his family was due to Abraham's faith and prayers of intercession for them. The angels told Lot, "We can't do anything until you're out of this place." Someone had interceded on their behalf to God, and I'm sure it was Abraham. As this story continues in Genesis 19, we find further evidence that angels who appear on the earth don't look like glorious angelic creatures all the time.

GENESIS 19:1–2

1 And there came two angels to Sodom at even; and Lot sat in the gate of Sodom: and Lot seeing them rose up to meet them; and he bowed himself with his face toward the ground;

2 And he said, Behold now, my lords, turn in, I pray you, into your servant's house, and tarry all night, and wash your feet.

LOT'S GRACIOUS WELCOME

Lot had the same kind of godly hospitality toward strangers in his heart that he had learned from Abraham. He said further:

GENESIS 19:2–5

2 And ye shall rise up early, and go on your ways. And they said, Nay; but we will abide in the street all night.

3 And he pressed upon them greatly; and they turned in unto him, and entered into his house, and he made them a feast, and did bake unleavened bread, and they did eat.

4 But before they lay down, the men of the city, even the men of Sodom, compassed the house round, both old and young, all the people from every quarter:

5 And they called unto Lot, and said unto him, Where are the men which came in to thee this night?. bring them out unto us, that we may know them.

HOMOSEXUAL ADVANCES

The men of Sodom were long gone in the direction of homosexuality. They wanted to have sex with the strangers who, in this case, were angels!

GENESIS 19:6–7

6 And Lot went out at the door unto them, and shut the door after him,

7 And said, I pray you, brethren, do not so wickedly.

If the two strangers had entered the town in all of their glory as angels, the request would not have been made at all. However, they appeared as normal, healthy males, which allowed the immoral response from the men of Sodom.

We also see that these two angels used their supernatural abilities to protect Lot and his family and deliver them out of the city.

THE GENTILE WHO WANTED TO KNOW GOD

Acts chapter 10 tells the story of an upright Gentile, a Roman centurion named Cornelius, who was earnestly seeking God. Cornelius was not saved, and he wanted to know God.

What can an angel do for someone who is seeking to know God? The angel can't do it himself, because he is not commissioned to do so. However, he can put that person in contact with someone who knows how to introduce him to God.

This is what happened to Cornelius. He was visited and given information by an angel.

ACTS 10:1–6

1 There was a certain man in Caesarea called Cornelius, a centurion of the band called the Italian band.

2 A devout man, and one that feared God with all his house, which gave much alms to the people, and prayed to God alway.

3 *He saw in a vision* evidently about the ninth hour of the day an *angel of God coming in to him,* and saying unto him, Cornelius.

4 And when he looked on him, he was afraid, and said, What is it, Lord? And he said unto him, Thy prayers and thine alms are come up for a memorial before God.

5 And now send men to Joppa, and call for one Simon, whose surname is Peter.

6 He lodgeth with one Simon a tanner, whose house is by the sea side: he shall tell thee what thou oughtest to do.

The angel told Cornelius exactly where Peter was and how to find him. An angel can put you who know the Gospel with someone who is seeking to know the Gospel, or he can direct that person who is seeking to you. We call these things "divine appointments." God makes divine appointments, and angels are the means He uses.

5

THE PROTECTION ANGELS PROVIDE

Everything angels do for you has one overall purpose: *to help bring to pass God's purpose for your life.*

However you are blessed by God in functioning in the Body of Christ—however you are gifted, or however you are operating according to God's calling and direction—angels will help you. They operate on earth for that purpose.

In Genesis 28, Jacob had a dream, and in the dream he saw a ladder that reached from Earth to Heaven:

GENESIS 28:12–14
12 And he dreamed, and behold a ladder set up on the earth, and the top of it reached to heaven: and behold the angels of God ascending and descending on it.
13 And, behold, the Lord stood above it, and said, I am the Lord God of Abraham thy father, and the God of Isaac: the land whereon thou liest, to thee will I give it, and to thy seed;
14 And thy seed shall be as the dust of the earth, and thou shalt spread abroad to the west, and to the east, and to the north, and to the south: and in thee and in thy seed shall all the families of the earth be blessed.

THE UNFULFILLED COMMISSION

In other words, we are to fill up this earth with the Gospel of Jesus Christ. Everyone who is called of God has a part in this task, and angels are our helpers in accomplishing it.

I think one reason we have never fulfilled that commission and filled the whole earth with the Gospel is because we have not depended enough upon the help of angels.

Angels can help you do things you couldn't otherwise do. They can help you get to places you would never get to otherwise.

They can pull down barriers—just like the walls of Jericho—whether in the spirit world or the natural world. Who do you think knocked over the walls of Jericho? Joshua 6:20 says *"the wall fell down flat."* That wall didn't just drop into some hole in the ground; it fell down flat. It takes a lot of force to knock a thick city wall flat!

ANGELS AS MATCHMAKERS

In Genesis chapter 24, we see another example of the intervention of angels in the life of one of the patriarchs. Abraham sent his chief servant, Eliezer of Damascus, to his homeland to find a bride for Isaac, his son.

Abraham understood this principle of angels helping us. He understood that angels would help him accomplish what ever he did in the Earth. When he sent his oldest and most trusted servant to perform a task for him, Abraham under stood that the angels of God would go with him and help him.

GENESIS 24:7

7 The Lord God of heaven, which took me from my father's house, and from the land of my kindred, and which spake unto me, and that sware unto me, saying, Unto thy seed will I give this land; *he shall send his angel before thee,* and thou shalt take a wife unto my son from thence.

So Eliezer took ten camels from his master's herd and set out with some servants for the city of Nahor, keeping in mind his master's admonition: *"He shall send his angel before thee."*

After he had been welcomed into Rebekah's household, Eliezer explained that Abraham had told him:

GENESIS 24:40

40 The Lord, before whom I walk, will send his angel with thee, and prosper thy way; and thou shalt take a wife for my son of my kindred, and of my father's house.

ANGELS MAKE YOU SUCCESSFUL

The angel will make your way prosperous! Angels will make you successful! Often we need supernatural help to be successful in this world. We can't become successful according to natural knowledge.

In verse 40, Eliezer told what happened when he met Rebekah at the well. He asked her for a little drink of water, and she not only offered water to him; she offered to draw water for all his camels! Imagine how thirsty ten camels were after crossing the desert for days without anything to drink! They would have drunk copious amounts of water.

Rebekah drew all that water out of the well with a pitcher for beasts which stank to high heaven. They may have even bitten and kicked her while she went about her task!

Sometimes you have to do things that aren't pleasant, but if you will submit to God like Rebekah did, a great reward will come at the end. *The same camels Rebekah watered carried her to Isaac!* (There is a wonderful allegory in this whole twenty-fourth chapter.)

THE ANGEL'S ROLE

Eliezer said the angel had helped him find the right girl. The angel put Rebekah in contact with Eliezer and Eliezer in contact with Rebekah.

I don't know how many young women were dwelling in the city of Nahor at that time, but there must have been a great many; and I don't know how many young women lived in Bethuel's household at that time, but I'm sure there were many there, too.

The angel put Abraham's servant in touch with the one young woman who was destined to be Isaac's bride. When her family asked her if she was willing to journey to another country to become the bride of a man she had never met, she said yes. She had to have had faith that God had ordained this "divine appointment" with Eliezer to give her consent. After all, she had never laid eyes on Isaac!

How many girls today would want to marry someone they had never met? They certainly would have to believe God meant them no harm. They would have to believe He is a good God. They would have to believe He was going to meet all their expectations and then some. Rebekah believed that.

The angel put this servant in touch with the right young woman. That's what God's angels will help you do. They will put you in touch with the people you need to meet to accomplish what God has given you to do. They will make divine appointments for you. The purpose of all of this is to spread the Gospel to the north, the south, the east, and the west—to fill the whole earth with the Gospel.

DEALING FOOLISHLY WITH ANGELS

Everything else angels do that has an impact on us personally and blesses us is so we will be a blessing. When God said He will bless us, it is so we will be a blessing, not just so we can heap up treasures on earth for ourselves.

It is not so we can say, "Angels, go get me a hundred oil wells," or "Okay, angels, go get me a ton of gold." I've heard people get into foolishness like that. Flesh, flesh, flesh—that's all it is!

If your purpose is to accomplish what God gave you to do, the angels will help you, and you will have an abundance for yourself. If you seek *first* the kingdom of God and His righteousness, as the Bible promises, all these other things will be added to you. And that's the order in which it happens.

So if your heart is to do God's will and seek His righteousness, you will be abundantly provided for, and that abundance will bless you and others. As we continue this study, bear this principle in mind, because it is behind everything else.

OBEDIENCE TO THE WORD

Angels go forth in obedience to the spoken Word. We saw that in Psalm 103:20: *"Bless the Lord, ye his angels, that excel in strength, that do his commandments, hearkening unto the voice of his word."*

Angels do God's commandments, hearkening unto the voice of His Word. *The Word is what they hearken to.* You and I are those who speak and live that Word.

Your *lifestyle* has just as loud a "voice" as the words you *say*—and sometimes louder. I wouldn't argue about which is the louder voice; I would simply say that both are extremely important.

What you say out of your mouth can only be effectual, however, if your lifestyle agrees with what you say. So both your lifestyle and your words have a voice, and the angels hearken to them.

PROTECTION IN THE NATURAL REALM

The next thing angels do in obedience to the spoken Word is to protect you in the natural realm. The same Psalm says that God redeems your natural life from destruction (Psalm 103:4).

Are you redeemed from spiritual death? Certainly you are. Jesus has already redeemed your *spiritual* life from destruction.

Angels will help you walk in the light of that salvation, and they will also redeem your *natural* life from destruction, because you have an enemy that seeks to steal, to kill, and to destroy you (John 10:10). Because your enemy is up to that, the angels act to keep him from succeeding.

If the devil is such a big bad dude, we would all be dead, wouldn't we? His will for your life is to end it prematurely! But God's will is that you fulfill all your days, finish your course and race, and be satisfied with the long life He promised you in Psalm 91 and reiterated over and over again in the New Testament.

PROTECTION FROM SPIRITS

We will look at a few passages of scripture that promise this. Psalm 35 is one of the strongest passages of scripture that promises protection where you need it most: from spirits in the spirit world. You need protection and the help of angels from the working of other spirits. They are trying to destroy you in the natural realm.

Many of you have been delivered from things you never knew had been plotted against you! In other cases, you did realize it. You didn't see the angels working on your behalf, but you knew God had protected you, and now you know angels were involved in it.

An example of this happened a few years ago to my wife, June. She came to an intersection that has four-way stop signs, and stopped. Suddenly a van came barreling through the intersection without even slowing down.

A woman who had stopped going south didn't see the van, and she pulled out in front of it as it barreled through the intersection. A horrendous crash followed. The van careened out of control and went around my wife's car on one side, and the woman driver's car went around her on the other side.

Little fragments of glass were scattered all over June's car—it took me forever to pick them off—but neither car touched hers!

The accident happened so quickly, she didn't have time to pray or say, "Help me, Lord!"

THE WORLD'S SHORTEST PRAYER

The world's shortest prayer is "Help!" God knows where it's coming from. What you need to do, however, is to stay full of the knowledge of God's protection and live in the overflow of it. Then, when unexpected things happen, you're already protected. You're not trying to build a hedge of protection; the hedge *already* surrounds you.

The devil is the one who is trying to see to it that your life doesn't complete its course, but his weapons won't prosper if you are full of the Word of God, living in the secret place of the most high God.

When you say things like *"The angel of the Lord encampeth round about them that fear him, and delivereth them"* from your heart, you commission angels. They are out there working for you.

WHERE YOUR BATTLE IS WON

Don't *neglect* such a great salvation, it says in Hebrews 2:3. Don't *forget* it, Psalm 103 says. Neglecting it or forgetting it would be the same thing. *Be mindful of the protection God has provided for you in every area.*

PSALM 35:1–2

1 Plead my cause, O Lord, with them that strive with me: fight against them that fight against me.
2 Take hold of shield and buckler, and stand up for mine help.

There will be a manifestation of this protection in the natural realm, but it begins in the spirit world. Remember, *the spirit realm is where your battle is won!* Think in terms of spirit beings, God's angels at work for you.

PSALM 35:3–5

3 Draw out also the spear, and stop the way against them that persecute me: say unto my soul, I am thy salvation.
4 Let them be confounded and put to shame that seek after my soul: let them be turned back and brought to confusion that devise my hurt.
5 Let them be as chaff before the wind: and *let the angel of the Lord chase them.*

MAKE SATAN PAY!

The angel of the Lord will chase away those spirits that seek to do you harm. He will put them to flight from doing what they have set out to do, because you continually believe what the Word of God says. In other words, it isn't going to be pleasant for those spirits! They are going to wish they had never picked on you.

Like a young preacher once said, "Make Satan pay!" That's true. It's all right to take vengeance in the spirit realm, because that realm has already been judged. Those spirits don't have any business coming around harassing you, because Jesus has redeemed you from their power!

They are trespassing on your territory when they come around you. Drive them off with the Word of God. Let your light shine, and realize that when you speak the Word according to your godly lifestyle, angels of God—a whole host of them, if necessary—will go into action on your behalf, chasing other spirits away and intervening for you in the natural realm.

PSALM 35:6–7

6 Let their way be dark and slippery: and *let the angel of the Lord persecute them.*

7 For without cause have they hid for me their net in a pit, which without cause they have digged for my soul.

HOW TO RECEIVE ANGELIC PROTECTION

Psalm 34:1–7 ties together what we should do in order to receive this angelic protection:

PSALM 34:1–7

1 I will bless the Lord at all times: his praise shall continually [not only in emergencies] be in my mouth.

2 My soul shall make her boast in the Lord: the humble shall hear thereof, and be glad.

3 O magnify the Lord [not the problem] with me, and let us exalt his name together.

4 I sought the Lord, and he heard me, and delivered me from all my fears.

5 They looked unto him, and were lightened: and their faces were not ashamed.

6 This poor man cried [this man who was unable to do for himself what angelic protection can provide], and the Lord healed him, and saved him out of all his troubles.

7 The angel of the Lord encampeth round about them· that fear him, and delivereth them.

SAVED FROM THE BURNING FIERY FURNACE

Shadrach, Meshach, and Abednego, whose story is told in the Book of Daniel, were a threesome who could attest to angelic protection. These young Jewish exiles were saved out of all their troubles—a burning fiery furnace in Babylon—by the angel of the Lord!

When they refused to bow down and worship a golden image set up by Nebuchadnezzar, the king became livid and threatened to throw them into a fiery furnace if they did not comply with his orders.

He commanded them to be brought before him, and Daniel 3:13 says he was full of rage and fury. How would you like to stand before the king of the whole empire when he is full of rage and fury—and *you're* the reason why he's so mad?

I used to work for some generals in the Air Force. Every morning I had to brief them about a program we were operating in the war in Vietnam, telling them how successful or unsuccessful it had been for whatever reason.

FULL OF RAGE AND FURY

Some days things didn't go the way these generals wanted them to. I can remember standing before a few of them who were like Nebuchadnezzar. They would already be full of rage and fury at seven o'clock in the morning!

I had been saved and filled with the Holy Spirit by the time I got that job, and God always comforted me in those situations. He told me I wasn't to be overly impressed when people didn't act right.

"They're just other human beings," He said. "Even if they have a great position, and even if it seems like they can make things bad for you, that's only what it seems like. You've got something they don't even know about working for you."

Nebuchadnezzar didn't know yet what was working on behalf of Shadrach, Meshach, and Abednego when he had them brought before him. He asked them:

DANIEL 3:14–15

14 Is it true . . . do not ye serve my gods, nor worship the golden image which I have set up?
15 Now if ye be ready that at what time ye hear the sound of . . . all kinds of musick, ye fall down and worship the image which I have made; well: but if ye worship not, ye shall be cast the same hour into the midst of a burning fiery furnace; and who is that God that shall deliver you out of my hands?

FAITH REPLIES

The king was about to find out who that God is! The three Hebrew youths answered him:

DANIEL 3:16–18

16 O Nebuchadnezzar, we are not careful to answer thee in this matter.

17 If it be so, our God whom we serve is able to deliver us from the burning fiery furnace, and he will deliver us out of thine hand, O king.

18 But if not, be it known unto thee, O king, that we will not serve thy gods, nor worship the golden image which thou hast set up.

In other words, they said, "O king, we are not nervous about your threat. We are not going to mince words for you. *If it be so*—if you throw us into the burning fiery furnace—our God is able, and He will deliver us."

The next three words, *"but if not,"* are often misunderstood to mean, "But if He doesn't deliver us." That's not what they mean at all. The three Hebrews had already *said* what God would do. They already *knew* what He would do. They said in faith, "Our God is able, and He *will* deliver us if you throw us into the furnace." There was no question about it in their minds.

DON'T VACILLATE

It is not faith to say, "But if He doesn't." You can't be wishy-washy and vacillate back and forth in your confession. You've got to *know* what your God will do. You've got to be persuaded of what He will do.

You can't say, "Well, our God *could*, but maybe He *won't*." You will never get any results with that attitude. No one in the Bible ever did.

They said, *"But if not, be it known unto thee, O king, that we will not serve thy gods, nor worship the golden image."* Think about that. If the threesome were thrown into the furnace and God *didn't* deliver them, they surely wouldn't live to worship any idols. They would be burned to a crisp. They would be dead!

So what does the phrase "but if not" refer to? It doesn't refer to whether or not God will deliver; it refers to whether or not the king will throw them into the furnace.

"When You Pass Through the Fire"

Therefore, when they said, "But if not," they weren't referring to whether or not the king's furnace would kill them. They didn't believe it would. They believed they would be delivered out of it.

They believed what Isaiah said: *"When thou walkest through the fire, thou shalt not be burned; neither shall the flame kindle upon thee"* (Isa. 43:2). They believed the 91st Psalm, which says, *"I will be with him in trouble; I will deliver him, and honour him"* (Psalm 91:15). That's what they believed.

So the "but if not" phrase does not refer to whether they get *burned up* or not; it refers to whether they get thrown in or not. "If you're good to us and don't throw us in, we're still not going to bow down and worship your idol" is what they were saying to the king.

You must be fully persuaded of these things. You cannot be of two minds about this. You won't receive what you ask for if you are. God cannot bless a double-minded person. *"Let not that person think that he shall receive any thing of the Lord,"* it says in James 1:7–8, because *"a double minded man is unstable in all his ways."*

Seven Times Hotter

When the three Hebrews refused to worship the golden idol, the king was so angry, he had the furnace heated seven times hotter than usual; and the men who threw the three young men into that furnace died when they got close to the fire. That's how hot it was.

DANIEL 3:19–20, 22–25

19 Then was Nebuchadnezzar full of fury, and the form of his visage was changed against Shadrach, Meshach, and Abednego: therefore he spake, and commanded that they should heat the furnace one seven times more than it was wont to be heated.

20 And he commanded the most mighty men that were in his army to bind Shadrach, Meshach, and Abednego, and to cast them into the burning fiery furnace.

22 Therefore because the king's commandment was urgent, and the furnace exceeding hot, the flame of the fire slew those men that took up Shadrach, Meshach, and Abednego.

23 And these three men . . . fell down bound into the midst of the burning fiery furnace.

24 Then Nebuchadnezzar the king was astonied, and rose up in haste, and spake, and said unto his counsellors, Did not we cast *three* men bound into the midst of the fire? They answered and said unto the king, True, O king.

25 He answered and said, Lo, I see *four* men loose, walking in the midst of the fire, and they have no hurt; *and the form of the fourth is like the Son of God.*

A KING HAS A CHANGE OF HEART

A few minutes ago, the king was so mad he couldn't speak. Now he's prophesying! God can change things. He changed this man. You can see he changed this man.

DANIEL 3:26–29

26 Then Nebuchadnezzar came near to the mouth of the burning fiery furnace, and spake, and said, Shadrach, Meshach, and Abednego, ye servants of the most high God, come forth, and come hither. Then Shadrach, Meshach, and Abednego, came forth out of the midst of the fire.

27 And the princes, governors, and captains, and the king's counsellors, being gathered together, saw these men, upon whose bodies the fire had no power, nor was an hair of their head singed, neither were their coats changed, nor the smell of fire had passed on them.

28 Then Nebuchadnezzar spake, and said, Blessed be the God of Shadrach, Meshach, and Abednego, *who hath sent his angel,* and *delivered his servants* that trusted in him, and have *changed the king's word,* and yielded their bodies, that they might not serve nor worship any god, except their own God.

29 There is no other God that can deliver after this sort.

The king changed his tune, didn't he? A lot of people will change theirs because of your testimony, when they see God working on your behalf. Nebuchadnezzar honored and promoted Shadrach, Meshach, and Abednego in his kingdom because of their faith and because of what he saw God do for them.

DANIEL'S TRIALS AND TRIBULATIONS

Daniel was a chief adviser to King Darius. Because he was wise and acted wisely, the king valued him. But in Daniel chapter 6, we find that King Darius was tricked by his counselors, who hated Daniel, were jealous of Daniel, and wanted Daniel's position for themselves.

They plotted to get rid of him, and they tricked the king into signing an irrevocable edict *"that whosoever shall ask a petition of any God or man for thirty days, save of thee, O king, he shall be cast into the den of lions"* (Dan. 6:7).

Once the king understood he had been tricked, he stayed up all night, pondering how he could deliver Daniel from having to go into the lions' den, but he couldn't come up with a solution. And, once given, there was no way he could change his word.

Daniel, on his part, did what he always did. He went into his house and knelt three times a day in prayer and thanksgiving. That was his lifestyle; prayer was part of his lifestyle.

THE KING'S TESTIMONY

The king knew God would deliver Daniel, because he served Him continually. Listen to what the king said in verse 16. It's a good testimony:

DANIEL 6:16–20

16 Then the king commanded, and they brought Daniel, and cast him into the den of lions. Now the king spake and said unto Daniel, Thy God whom thou servest continually, he will deliver thee.

17 So a stone was brought, and laid upon the mouth of the den; and the king sealed it with his own signet, and with the signet of his lords; that the purpose might not be changed concerning Daniel.

18 Then the king went to his palace, and passed the night fasting: neither were instruments of music brought before him: and his sleep went from him.

19 Then the king arose very early in the morning, and went in haste unto the
den of lions.

20 And when he came to the den, he cried with a lamentable voice unto Daniel:
and the king spake and said to Daniel, O Daniel, servant of the living God, is
thy God, whom thou servest continually, able to deliver thee from the lions?

DANIEL'S TESTIMONY

I've often thought Daniel could have made the king sweat a little if
he didn't answer him immediately, but Daniel didn't belittle or attack
him. He didn't ask, "What's the matter with you? Why did you sign
such a stupid edict?"

Instead, he treated the king with respect, like he always did. He
said:

21 O king, live for ever.
22 My God hath sent his angel, and hath shut the lions' mouths.

Those lions were hungry! They would have devoured him in a minute, just like they had devoured earlier victims, but they didn't. Daniel
spent the night in there with all those ferocious beasts and reported:

DANIEL 6:22–24
22 They have not hurt me: for as much as before him [before Daniel's God]
innocency was found in me; and also before thee, O king, have I done no
hurt.

23 Then was the king exceeding glad for him, and commanded that they should
take Daniel up out of the den. So Daniel was taken up out of the den, and no
manner of hurt was found upon him, because he believed in his God.

24 And the king commanded, and they brought those men which had accused
Daniel, and they cast them into the den of lions.

GOD'S VENGEANCE

They cast all who had accused Daniel falsely with their wives and
children into the den of lions. They were immediately torn into pieces.
Daniel had spent the whole night in there and emerged without a
scratch. The angel of God came and saw to that!

The Bible says if you dig a pit for your brother, you will fall into it yourself. If you try to trap or hurt someone else, it will come back on you. If you throw a stone, it will fall on you.

A man named Haman built a gallows on which to hang Mordecai, according to the account in the Book of Esther. Who was hanged on Haman's fifty-cubit-high gallows? Haman. That should be a lesson to us not to take vengeance upon flesh and blood. Vengeance is God's, not ours, as far as human beings are concerned.

PETER NEEDED HELP

Peter found himself in deep trouble in Acts chapter 12. He had been captured by King Herod, who was planning to kill him after the Passover. The king planned to take Peter before the people and kill him, because he thought the people would enjoy it.

ACTS 12:5–7

5 Peter therefore was kept in prison: but prayer was made without ceasing of the church unto God for him.

6 And when Herod would have brought him forth, the same night Peter was sleeping between two soldiers, bound with two chains: and the keepers before the door kept the prison.

7 And, behold, *the angel of the Lord came upon him,* and a light shined in the prison: and he smote Peter on the side, and raised him up, saying, Rise up quickly. And his chains fell off from his hands.

That's something you can't do for yourself! If you're bound with chains in the middle of a prison, you can't say, "Chains, fall off!" Without angelic help, it won't happen.

YOU NEED ANGELS, TOO

I think many people miss this point. They say, "I don't need any angels. Just me and God—that's enough. I can do it all by faith."

What if God ordained that faith is the way angels minister for you, and He has appointed them to minister for you? Would it be all right then if they helped you? I think it would be more than all right, don't you?

Why did Peter need angelic help? Why didn't his chains fall off *before* the angel came? When the angel appeared, smote him on the side, and said, "Rise up quickly," they fell off his hands.

Peter was about like I am when he was awakened in the middle of the night. He didn't function well mentally at first. The angel had to tell him, *"Gird thyself, and bind on your sandals"* (Acts 12:8).

After he did, the angel continued, *"Cast thy garment about thee, and follow me"* (v. 8). The angel had to treat him like a little kid, saying, "Put your coat on, Peter, and follow me." This was because Peter was still half asleep, and he thought he was dreaming:

ACTS 12:9–10
9　And he went out, and followed him; and wist not that it was true which was done by the angel; but thought he saw a vision.
10　When they were past the first and the second ward, they came unto the iron gate that leadeth unto the city; which opened to them of his own accord.

ANGEL POWER

That's another thing that doesn't happen routinely: Iron gates locked shut don't swing open for you just because you pass by. The angel did that. It's not difficult for angels to do things like that. If there had been fifty padlocks on the gates, they would still have swung open easily for the angel.

ACTS 12:10–11
10　And they went out, and passed on through one street; and forthwith the angel departed from him.
11　And when Peter was come to himself, he said, Now I know of a surety, that the Lord hath sent his angel, and hath delivered me out of the hand of Herod, and from all the expectation of the people of the Jews.

In other words, no matter what formal, cold religious people decided to do to him, Peter said he knew he was delivered from all of it—*all* of it—by the angel of the Lord.

No Lack of Deliverance

Let's look again and see what Psalm 34:6 says: *"This poor man cried, and the Lord heard him, and saved him out of all his troubles."*

How is this man saved out of all his troubles? The answer is found in verse 7: *"The angel of the Lord encampeth round about them that fear him, and delivereth them."*

"See for yourself," we are exhorted in verses 8 and 9: *"O taste and see that the Lord is good: blessed is the man that trusteth in him. O fear the Lord, ye his saints: for there is no want to them that fear him."*

There is no want or lack for deliverance to them that fear God. No matter what weapon has been formed against you, it will not prosper.

Psalm 34 goes on to talk about keeping your tongue from evil and your lips from speaking guile, departing from evil, doing good, seeking and pursuing peace—all the things a Christian should have in his or her lifestyle.

So the angel of the Lord is encamped round about you. Angels are "happy campers" when they see you walk in the light of God's Word. There is nothing they like better than to see you believe the Word of God.

When do you have to believe the Word? When you're in the midst of a test, a trial, or a temptation—or even a burning fiery furnace!

Anyone can live an overcoming life when nothing bad is going on in your life, but the angels really rejoice when you choose to believe God during an attack by the enemy. That's when they go to work on your behalf.

Delivered From a Fiery Plane Crash!

In 1977, a man named Norman Williams wrote a book entitled *Terror at Tenerife*, which described his escape from the worst airplane crash in the history of aviation to that time.

Mr. Williams wrote the book with George Otis as a testimony of how God had delivered him from that fiery plane crash. It happened on March 27, 1977 and cost 576 lives. Mr. Williams was one of only 67 survivors.

Mr. Williams was planning a business trip to Europe. He was a scheduled passenger on a Pan American Airways 747 flight, and his first stop was to be Spain.

Several days before he left, his mother asked him to come and pray with her. She was a Pentecostal woman who had prayed Heaven and earth together on many occasions. She told him she had an urgency in her spirit that they pray together before he left.

During their time of prayer, she began to weep almost convulsively, and he had to finish the prayer. "I had never seen my mother cry," he recalled.

She didn't tell him to stay home, and she didn't tell him, "Don't go." However, she said, "Before you go on this trip, get in the Word of God and build yourself up concerning God's angels and His protection for you. Get in the 91st Psalm especially," so he did.

Psalm 91 promises, *"A thousand shall fall at thy side, and ten thousand at your right hand; but it shall not come nigh thee"* (v. 7).

FLIGHT DIVERTED

Mr. Williams boarded the Pan Am 747. It was full of people. Because of a bomb threat, the airplane was diverted to the Canary Islands, Tenerife being one of them.

They landed on a little-used auxiliary field which had a control tower and little else. During their long delay, the weather turned from bright and sunny to foggy.

Another 747, a KLM Royal Dutch Airliner, also loaded with people, had been diverted to Tenerife. It took on 142,000 pounds of extra fuel during the lengthy delay.

Finally the Pan Am crew started the engines on their plane and received permission to begin taxiing out to the active runway.

A Pilot's Tragic Error

The KLM airplane had already taxied to the end of the active runway, made a 180-degree turn, and was now headed back down the runway preparing for takeoff. Apparently the KLM pilot thought the call clearing Pan Am to proceed down the runway was *his* clearance to take off, so he started rolling down that active runway toward the Pan Am airplane, accelerating to 180 miles per hour!

Visibility was about a quarter of a mile. By the time the KLM plane had gone a quarter of a mile, its pilot saw the Pan Am airplane right in front of him! He tried to fly over it, but he couldn't make it. Slow speed and the extra fuel weight caused the KLM plane to lift off and climb slowly, and the extra fuel caused the wings of the KLM airplane to flex.

The Pan Am pilot, who survived, said he was "shocked beyond belief" at the sight of another airplane coming toward them.

The KLM jet lifted off the ground a little, but it plowed head on into the Pan Am plane. Everyone on the KLM plane was killed. The Pan Am plane was cut in half.

Thanking God for Protection

Mr. Williams had no idea anything was about to happen, but he had been doing what his mother told him to do: He was praying and confessing the Word of God over himself and thanking God for protecting him.

All of a sudden, a horrendous crash occurred, followed by explosions. People all around him were burning to death, screaming, crying, and cursing. "They began to melt just like wax mannequins," Mr. Williams said. "The scene of our prayers in my mother's living room became alive. My mind was taken over by scripture."

Fighting his way through the inferno, he said, "I stand on the Word! I stand on the Word!" The aluminum on the air plane began liquefying. A large object came hurling toward him. He pushed it aside, saying, "In the Name of Jesus!"

Then he saw a jagged hole in the ceiling, 15 feet above him. He was 52 years old and 260 pounds at the time, and in the natural he could not have leaped that high—but he suddenly found himself being propelled out of the hole as the plane continued to explode.

He landed on a wing and then jumped the equivalent of three stories to the ground, joining the handful of other survivors who were frantically attempting to crawl through the grass to safety. He had been in the middle of an inferno, but his clothes were not even burned! At this point, the remnant of the airplane was totally engulfed in flames and was gutted within about three minutes.

"I realized what God had done for me in the midst of that furnace of fire," Mr. Williams says. "I should have died, and I realized it. God spared my life to share the message of His deliverance."

ANGELS TO THE RESCUE

How did he get to the wing? Angels took him out of that burning inferno—right through it in an instant—and put him out there in a safe place, sitting on the wing tip!

You can have the same protection Mr. Williams had, but you've got to do what he did. You've got to immerse yourself in the Word of God. As it says in Hebrews 2:3, *"How shall we escape, if we neglect so great salvation."* And Psalm 103:2 says, *"Forget not all of his benefits."* Be mindful of them. Stay in contact with them.

You can't wait for a tragedy or accident like that to happen and then start trying to believe at that point. How could you? There is no time.

ESCAPE ON A MOUNTAINSIDE

Years ago, I was driving a truck, pulling my own little travel trailer through Montana, and my family was in the truck. We were going up a roadbed where Interstate 90 is now. The old highway was still in use then, but they were building up its roadbed to build the interstate highway on it.

We got to a certain area in the country where the road started to climb over a ridge and up a big mountain. The roadbed, which had been built up about 20 feet, went through a marshy low area. One lane was gravel and the other was a completed lane of paved interstate. They handled the two lanes of traffic.

Traffic was stopped for about 30 minutes while they worked on the road. I was the first driver of a long line of cars heading west. Up the hill about half a mile, an eighteen wheeler headed the other long line of vehicles.

Finally the road crew moved their heavy equipment out of the way and allowed traffic to resume from both directions at once. The eighteen-wheeler started down the hill, and I started up the hill. I guess he wasn't going fast enough to satisfy someone behind him, because about the time I approached the truck, someone tried to pass him! It was a blue '57 Chevrolet.

I'll never forget it. I can remember what it looked like to this very day. He just floored his car and tried to get around the truck—dust, rocks, and everything flying—before I got there, but his judgment was so bad I would have hit him right where the box and the tractor were joined together.

There was nowhere to go. The side of the road was 20 feet down. I decided, however, that going off the road would be better than having a head-on collision, so I turned the wheel to go "overboard." I fully intended to go over the side, but about the time I decided to do that, the driver of the Chevy decided to do the same thing.

So now we were going to have a midair collision somewhere out there in space. When I saw him turn his car out, I cranked the wheel of my truck back in. My trailer had already swung out of line, but I drove right between his car and that tractor-trailer—without touching anything.

The Chevy driver went sailing past me. He went down the road on the shoulder past about ten other cars and came to rest teetering on the edge of the embankment. I don't know what he was driving on out there!

I watched him in one of those big mirrors that are mounted on a bumper when you're pulling a trailer. I watched him drive all the way down there, and he never went over the edge. His wheels were over the edge, but he didn't go over the edge, and he didn't crash into anyone else.

I drove right between the truck and the car, praising God. I didn't have time to pray first as it happened, but I had prayed that morning before I started driving. I was in the Word, in the 91st Psalm, trusting what it said.

One second there was no way.

The next second there was a way.

God made the way, hallelujah! His angels acted supernaturally to prevent a calamity.

6

DELIVERED FROM DESTRUCTION

Sometimes I think people react too much to outside influences, such as times when the world forms a weapon against them. They want to fight it, but there really isn't any fight they can win in the flesh.

Why? Because it isn't in the *natural* realm, or the realm of flesh and blood, that we wrestle, overcome, or prevail. The only way we will have victory in that realm is when we battle in the *spirit* world or realm, fighting the good fight of faith there.

In other words, we don't gain victory over flesh and blood by contending with flesh and blood in a natural way. But we do get victory by taking hold of God's promise in Isaiah 54:17, which says, *"No weapon that is formed against thee shall prosper; and every tongue that shall rise up against thee in judgment thou shalt condemn."*

This means you would condemn the charges made against you. You would show them to be faulty and non-productive by your lifestyle, your agreeing with God's Word, and your submission to God in that time of trial.

When other people don't agree with you, that's the time you want to agree most with God. Don't fight them. Just hang on to what God said. God will vindicate you. God will demonstrate that you are the righteous one. And the ministry of angelic beings will be involved in your vindication.

THE REALM OF PROTECTION

You would probably say that *protection* is the greatest benefit of their involvement in your trial, but *vindication* is another benefit of it. God will vindicate you, and angelic beings will help you. They will touch what needs to be touched in the natural realm, according to God's commandment.

We don't know how to judge or how to do it. We would make mistakes in doing so. If it were up to us to decide who lives and dies, we would make the wrong choices. Because God knows a lot more than we do, He is the only One Who can make such choices correctly.

Remember this concerning the realm of protection: "The angel of the Lord encampeth round about them that fear him to deliver them." To do what? To *deliver* them.

Overcoming Faith

Peter was in prison, facing execution by beheading the next day, but he was sound asleep. He wasn't worried! There is no such thing as nervous faith. That doesn't mean your nerves won't jangle once in a while, but don't let that nervous jangle determine your actions and your thinking. Keep centered on the Word of God. Don't let opposition move you. Only be moved by the Word of God.

Smith Wigglesworth had a way of saying plainly, "I don't let Smith tell me how I feel. I tell Smith how I feel." In other words, he didn't let his flesh tell him how he was going to feel that day; he told his flesh how to feel.

Sometimes you must command your own flesh, "Get in line with the Word of God."

When upsetting or disastrous events that don't line up with the Word of God happen around you, that's the wrong time to stop believing the Word. If, however, you have been believing the Word when those things happen, you will continue in the Word. So if being in the Word has been a regular pattern in your life when there have been no challenges to your faith, when a challenge comes, it will not seem so big to you.

Magnify God, and don't magnify events, problems, or challenges to faith. If you continually magnify God, everything contrary to His Word will no longer look so overwhelming.

PRAYERS FOR PROTECTION

There was a time in my own life before I was saved that God moved to preserve my life. I really believe someone was praying for me. I believe someone asked God to be merciful to me.

I don't know if you have ever been awakened in the middle of the night to pray. Sometimes you may know what it is about, and sometimes you won't know what it was about. However, if you will just pray in other tongues, you will finally pray through.

You can thank God that He is doing something good for someone, because He used you as a believer in covenant relationship to pray through something for someone who wasn't able to pray for himself or herself.

It might be a believer, or it might be an unbeliever, but whoever it was, that person's name is written in the Lamb's Book of Life, whether he is a believer yet or not. And he still needs prayer.

I joined the Air Force when I was19 years old. I learned how to fly jet airplanes, and I did that until I left the service 23 years later. The first jet I flew was a fighter aircraft, an F-86F, a Sabre jet from the Korean War era.

FLYING OVER LIBYA

After the Korean War, our unit was stationed in Europe, and we went to North Africa for gunnery training. Our whole unit was moved to Libya twice a year for a month. We practiced gunnery over the Mediterranean.

We shot at towed targets or air-to-air targets, and we also went out over the desert, where we practiced bombing, strafing, and so forth on an air-to-ground range.

One day I was in a flight of four airplanes practicing high-angle bombing practice for nuclear weapon delivery on that desert range. A small nuclear weapon that we could deliver with that airplane would be hung under the wing in event of war.

Of course, if you are going to detonate a nuclear weapon, you need to be a good distance from it when it goes off! Different kinds of delivery made it possible for us to deliver it on a target, but when it detonated, we would be far from the scene.

We came up over our target at 20,000 feet—four miles up—in this high-angle bombing practice. We rolled the airplane upside down. We pulled the nose back through that target until we were flying almost vertically. Then we reversed on it and held the sight on the target until we had it stabilized and then released the practice bomb.

In that dive, we gained a lot of air speed. We started at a low speed, but even with the throttle pulled back and the speed brakes out, we got up to about 600 miles an hour.

When we got to the right sight picture, at about 10,000 feet, we released our bomb and pulled out. Of course, we weren't releasing *real* nuclear weapons in our practices; we were releasing little three-pound practice bombs which had the same trajectory. We could drop six of them, one at a time, from a bomb rack under the wing on each mission.

BOMBING PRACTICE TURNS DANGEROUS

I was on my second or third run, and I got a little too close to the airplane ahead of me. We worked hard to keep the separation right, because if the pilot ahead of you was in his dive and you got right behind him and released your bomb, you might bomb *him*—and we didn't want to do that!

When we rolled in over the target, we called in on the target using the radio, and when we were about halfway through our pullout, we called off again so the pilot behind us could roll in. He was waiting for that call.

Perhaps I was a little close to the airplane in front of me, or that pilot was slow calling off, so I went a little farther over the target than normal.

I was flying the wing commander's airplane that day. It was painted like an Easter egg, with candy stripes around it and stars on the nose and tail. The wing commander was very proud of it. The ground crews kept it polished and cleaner than the rest of the planes. Whenever any of us flew it, we were aware of the wing commander's feelings, and we were careful not to scratch it or damage it in any way.

So I got right up over the target, and then I got a little past it by the time the other pilot called off. As I rolled in beyond the target, I had to pull the nose back farther and reverse it, and I was actually coming a little past vertical down on that target to keep the sight picture right.

I was pushing the stick forward a lot to do this. I didn't trim all the pressure off, and I was leaning forward in the seat, because of the negative angle, to look through the gun sight.

ALONG FOR THE RIDE

When I released the bomb and started to recover, the airplane seemed like it had swapped ends! I was leaning forward in the seat, and my head went right down between my feet. My hands came off the stick and the throttle and dangled down there with my head!

Suddenly I was just along for the ride! I didn't know where I was going. I wasn't too sure which *direction* the plane was headed anymore. It could have snapped at that point and headed straight for the ground, for all I knew.

A swept-wing airplane doesn't fly straight by itself. It turns one way or the other, but it won't go straight. So this plane was probably in a spiral, heading toward the ground! But I didn't know. At this point, I had become little more than a spectator with a bad view!

I was trying to push my head up as hard as I could, but I couldn't—it was down there on the floor of the airplane with my feet. I don't know how I escaped breaking my back, because I was wearing a heavy parachute and other equipment.

15 SECONDS TO THE GROUND!

The airplane was pulling a lot of G's. When you're going toward the ground from 10,000 feet at 600 miles an hour, it takes only 15 seconds to get there! The whole episode seemed like it took forever to me.

I pushed and pushed and pushed, but I couldn't get my head up. Finally, because the G force had lessened, I got my head up. I really didn't want to look, because if all you can see is *sand* at that point, you're not going to be able to do anything about it—it's too late. But I saw *blue sky*, praise the Lord!

I wasn't saved. I didn't know God. I didn't know Jesus as my personal Savior. That airplane had flown perfectly straight! It was upside down, high in the sky, starting to come across the top of what would have been a long loop. I recognized where I was and what I was doing, and I recovered the airplane and got it back straight and level.

When I looked at the instruments, just to check everything, the G meter reading almost made me eject, because it was registering on the maximum it could read!

There were three needles on the G meter. One records your current amount of G's. A "G" is one force of gravity, and you are sitting comfortably under one force of gravity right now. If you weigh 200 pounds and pull five G's, you effectively weigh 1,000 pounds.

And if you look in the rear view mirror in that jet when you're pulling five G's, your face doesn't look normal; you look weird, because your facial features droop.

More G's than that makes you look *really* weird. That kind of G force holds you down and keeps you from being able to sit up. I finally was able to sit up because the G force slacked off.

MAXED OUT

The current registering needle was sitting at one G, because the airplane was straight and level at that point. But there were two little needles that showed the maximum you had experienced, positive or negative. (Negative G's are registered when you are upside down.) That positive needle was on the maximum reading!

The airplane was built to withstand 7.3 G's positive or 3 G's negative. You could probably pull 8 and nothing major would happen. The top of the calibration on the G meter was 9 1/2, and there was a space beyond that and then a peg. *The needle was on the peg.* I would estimate it was registering more than 10 G's on that airplane.

The wings should have fallen off by then—but they didn't. Looking at that meter made me think they were about to, so I flew it *very carefully* back to our base in Tripoli. At that time, Libya was ruled by a king who was friendly to us and the British, and he allowed our armed forces to use the country for various missions.

PAMPERING THE "EASTER EGG"

I lowered the landing gear when I was still up at 15,000 feet, because I didn't want the seemingly weakened wings to fall off when I was too close to the ground. Nothing happened. The gear came down and locked normally. That was amazing to me. Something should have broken in the hydraulic system that operated the gear with that much G force on it, but it didn't.

I landed the airplane *very carefully*, turned off the active runway, called the tower, and said, "I'm going to park it right here. I don't want to taxi it in, because if it falls apart, I don't want to be sitting in it when it happens."

The line chief and the crew chief came out and looked in the cockpit. They asked, "What's the matter with the airplane, lieutenant?"

I said, "Look at the G meter." They looked at the G meter and said, "Oh! Don't move!" They had the same initial reaction I had that the airplane was about to fall apart. But it didn't.

They towed it in *very carefully*, took it to our field maintenance hanger, examined it from one end to the other—and found nothing wrong with it.

There were many little fuel lines, hydraulic lines, and such things that ran the length of the fuselage back around the tail that must have been under tremendous pressure, and they should have broken. Nothing broke.

NO DAMAGE

They looked over that plane for a whole week and found nothing wrong with it. They even sent some parts of it to the base lab to be analyzed for metal fatigue. Nothing was fatigued. I was amazed that I hadn't harmed my back when it was bent under so much G force, but my back didn't seem to be damaged. Nothing was damaged.

What made the airplane fly straight? What kept it from breaking up in flight? There is no explanation for it. People were scratching their heads for weeks trying to figure out why the airplane wasn't destroyed. I just thought, "Well, I'm lucky."

I remember saying, "Thank God, I'm all right," but that was just "religious" talk; it wasn't faith. People thank God all the time. The trouble is, they thank Him for half the things He *hasn't* done as well as the things He *has* done.

I never realized what had really happened until years later when I was studying the Bible about what angels do for us. They contact things in the natural realm that we need contacted, and they change things in the natural realm that would otherwise cause our destruction.

FALLING LIKE A ROCK

I've had other near-misses while flying. I once lost both engines while flying the SR-71A. At that time, I was saved, filled with the Holy Spirit, and beginning to be grounded in the Word of God.

We were going 2100 miles an hour at 85,000 feet. And when both engines flamed out, that airplane didn't glide in the direction of the ground; it fell like a rock!

I had to stick the nose down to get the air to flow through the inlets to relight the engines. I had attempted a restart a little higher than I should have, where the air was rather thin, because I wanted to get at least one of the engines running. The first two or three attempts on each engine with the nose down didn't work.

I told my navigator, "If it doesn't start *this* time, you and I are leaving this plane, because it's not going to take it long to get to the ground at this speed." But at about 35,000 feet, one engine did relight, and the rumble of that engine starting sure sounded good!

A pilot normally doesn't want to bail out of a $45 million airplane. It's more comfortable inside than it is outside, but we had a good ejection system if we needed it. We knew it would work, but we still didn't want to leave a $45 million airplane to crash. That was back in the sixties, when $45 million was a lot more than it is today.

THE ENGINE THAT SHOULDN'T HAVE STARTED

On the last attempt, the one engine rumbled and came to life, so we were able to fly the airplane home and land on its power, which was a great blessing. At first, it didn't look like the engine was going to start. All the natural reasons for it to start were not there. But it did start.

It would take too long to explain why both engines quit, but it had to do with what we call "unstarts." The air wasn't getting into the engines. All the inlet geometry that brought air in at that high speed broke on both engines.

In an unstart, the airplane is vibrating so rapidly you can't even read the instruments, and you're sitting way up on the end of that long fuselage, vibrating rapidly from side to side. You just grab for the restart switches and hope you get them and not something else.

I've had experiences like this over and over again. I would have died three times over if God hadn't done something. And my wife would probably be dead if she hadn't had angelic protection when both of those vehicles describèd in the last chapter were coming straight at her car. However, both spun around her car and didn't touch it.

So angels intervene and help believers or those who will be heirs of salvation and need supernatural assistance. It's not difficult for them. It's easy for them. That's their job. We can't do these things for ourselves, so they provide protection and deliverance for us.

GUARDIAN ANGELS

In Matthew 18:10, Jesus is speaking to His disciples about who is the greatest in God's kingdom. He uses a little child as His example, saying: *"Take heed that ye despise not one of these little ones; for I say unto you, That in heaven their angels do always behold the face of my Father which is in heaven."*

This phrase "their angels" is where we get the term "guardian angels" (or angel). It appears that we as children had at least one angel assigned to minister for us.

Here, as in any act of God for a person not yet born again through faith in Jesus Christ, we see that our Father sends forth angels to help us according to His foreknowledge that we are believers. Angels work to bless and help us overcome, even to the preserving of natural life itself.

THE CONDEMNED MAN SLEEPS

As we saw in Acts chapter 12, an angel appeared to Peter to deliver him out of prison. That action protected him, but it did more than that. Peter was a human being. How do you suppose *you* would feel the night before you were going to be executed? You would probably be restless—but Peter was sound asleep!

Perhaps the angels had already been helping him before one appeared to deliver him out of the prison. *Sometimes the ministry of angels and the ministry of the Holy Spirit are almost identical.* If you can't tell which is which, don't worry about it. They are God's angels, doing His commandments, and they are part of the working of the Spirit as well as the Holy Spirit Himself. Don't strive trying to identify which is which.

You can be confident that the working of angelic beings always agrees with God's Word, and the Holy Spirit always exalts the Word of God and Jesus. So do the angels of God.

COMFORT IN PRISON

Angels can bring comfort, aid, and direction to human beings. Peter got direction from the angel that visited him in prison. The angel had to tell him what to do, because Peter was still half asleep!

He told Peter to get up quickly, put on his sandals and cloak, and follow him. Peter wasn't able to do any of those things for himself. The angel also caused the chains to fall off his hands.

If you're going to have your head cut off the next day, it's comforting to get rescued from prison! The angel gave Peter assistance he couldn't provide for himself. His actions also implied deliverance and protection—and there was even more to it than that.

In Acts chapter 10, when Cornelius was calling on God, seeking to know Him, an angel appeared to him and gave him detailed directions how he could find Peter to preach the Gospel to his household.

It is important to remember that you should never pray to *angels* for direction; you should always pray only to *God* for direction.

Sometimes people get this mixed up, and they seek direction from angels. Don't do it! Nowhere in the Bible does it tell you to seek angels. Seek God. *Pray to the Father in Jesus' Name.* Then whatever direction is given to you is God's will for you.

You are not to pray, "O God, send an angel to direct me." An angel might direct you, but it won't be from God. *You open yourself up to deception when you do anything contrary to the Word of God.*

PHILIP'S PROPER RESPONSE

Sometimes we need angelic intervention because of unusual circumstances. At least these circumstances seem unusual to human beings.

How are you normally guided and led? In most things being led by the Holy Spirit in your spirit is sufficient. Most of the time, you are able to receive and understand that kind of direction, so that is how God guides you.

But sometimes unusual circumstances arise, and for you to be able to react in a timely fashion, it takes something more than being led by the Spirit in your spirit. We will examine one such case in Acts 8.

ACTS 8:5–8

5 Then Philip went down to the city of Samaria, and preached Christ unto them.

6 And the people with one accord gave heed unto those things which Philip spake, hearing and seeing the miracles which he did.

7 For unclean spirits, crying with loud voice, came out of many that were possessed with them: and many taken with palsies, and that were lame, were healed.

8 And there was great joy in that city.

God was at work in that revival. He was reaching the lost through Philip's preaching in a city of Samaria.

The chapter goes on to tell about Simon the sorcerer and how the apostles Peter and John were sent from Jerusalem to see the revival for themselves when they heard that the Samaritans had received the Word of God.

Peter and John laid hands on the new converts, prayed that they might receive the Holy Spirit, and they were baptized in the Holy Spirit.

While all this was going on, there was Philip in Samaria, preaching Jesus, and a great revival was occurring. But now God wanted him to leave that great move and go out in the desert to meet one man. It may be difficult for the natural man to receive instructions like that.

"IT'S THE DEVIL!"

If you are in the middle of a great citywide revival, with joy breaking forth all over the place and signs and wonders accompanying the Word you are preaching daily, it might be hard for you to receive God's direction, "Go out in the desert by yourself." You might even think you were hearing from the devil!

I have actually rebuked God more than once, thinking He was the devil talking to me! I'm sure it didn't offend Him; He doesn't take offense. In fact, He probably laughed, "That poor, pitiful thing. Here I am talking to him, and he thinks I am the devil!" But what He was saying was hard for me to receive in light of what He had already said to me.

I'll tell you how it happened. When I was first in the ministry, I was single. I had been married and divorced earlier in life, and I was told by God to quit looking for a wife. He said, "If you don't quit looking on your own terms, you're going to find the wrong one. Just relax. I'll bring you one."

So when I began to be interested in June, I thought it was the devil, and I rebuked him. But she wasn't from the devil; she was from God. Twenty years later, we're still very happy. But at first I thought the attraction was simply my own flesh. I rebuked it three or four times before I realized it wasn't going to go away.

If you really believe you have dominion over the devil and rebuke him, he will flee from you. If you understand you have absolute authority over him when you rebuke him, he's gone. So if the peaceable impression is still within you, it must not have been the devil.

INSTRUCTION FROM AN ANGEL

Philip had to be guided out of something very powerful—something he was responsible for and the leader of—and he had to believe it was God telling him to go out in the desert alone.

How did God guide him in this case? Verse 26 begins, *"The angel of the Lord spoke to Philip."* An angel sent by God spoke to Philip.

Why did God send an angel to speak to him at this point? Because it would be difficult for him to receive instruction by a simple inner witness that he should leave a mighty revival at that point in his spiritual development and understanding. Perhaps it wouldn't have been so difficult for someone else at a different point in his or her spiritual development.

The angel's message was:

ACTS 8:26–29

26 Arise, and go toward the south unto the way that goeth down from Jerusalem unto Gaza, which is desert.

27 And he arose and went and, behold, a man of Ethiopia, an eunuch of great authority under Candace queen of the Ethiopians, who had the charge of all her treasure, and had come to Jerusalem for to worship,

28 Was returning, and sitting in his chariot read Esaias [Isaiah] the prophet.

29 Then the Spirit said unto Philip....

BACK TO THE INNER WITNESS

Notice this time the angel didn't speak to Philip; the inner witness took over again. Realize from this excellent example that you are not going to have an angel follow you around for the rest of your life, telling you what to do.

If you have a visitation from an angel, it's because you needed it. Just thank God for the visitation, and go on and don't expect it to be a continual experience. That will not happen. But if you need it and God provides it, praise the Lord.

ACTS 8:29–30

29 Then the Spirit said unto Philip, Go near, and join thyself to this chariot.

30 And Philip ran thither to him.

You know the rest of the story, how Philip led the man to the Lord, baptized him in water, and then Philip was translated to Azotus, where he immediately resumed preaching, and the Ethiopian went on his way rejoicing. From historical evidence, that Samaritan revival did spread to Ethiopia, most likely through this eunuch.

ANGELIC ASSISTANCE

There are other places in the Bible where similar things happened. Because we are human beings, sometimes angelic visitations like this are necessary. Our humanity can be affected by circumstances. Nevertheless, we must keep our feelings under subjection to God's Word, and while we are doing that, sometimes we need assistance from angels.

Mark's Gospel records a story about someone who needed assistance.

MARK:9–13

9 And it came to pass in those days, that Jesus came from Nazareth of Galilee, and was baptized of John in Jordan.

10 And straightway coming up out of the water, he saw the heavens opened, and the Spirit like a dove descending upon him:

11 And there came a voice from heaven, saying, Thou art my beloved Son, in whom I am well pleased.

12 And immediately the spirit driveth him into the wilderness.

13 And he was there in the wilderness forty days, tempted of Satan; and with the wild beasts; *and the angels ministered unto him.*

If you had been fasting all that time and enduring temptations out there in the barren wilderness, surrounded by wild animals, you would need some ministry, too! Jesus did, and certainly you would. The Bible says angels ministered to Jesus, but it doesn't say what they did.

PAUL'S PERILOUS VOYAGE

In Acts chapter 27, we see how another man was ministered to by angels in an unusual set of circumstances. Paul was about to depart on a sea voyage. His destination was Rome. Luke, who accompanied him, tells their story.

ACTS 27:1–9

1 And when it was determined that we should sail into Italy, they delivered Paul and certain other prisoners unto one named Julius a centurion of Augustus' band.

2 And entering into a ship of Adramyttium, we launched, meaning to sail by the coasts of Asia; one Aristarchus, a Macedonian of Thessalonica, being with us.

3   And the next day we touched at Sidon. And Julius courteously entreated
    Paul, and gave him liberty to go unto his friends and refresh himself.

4   And when we had launched from thence, we sailed under Cyprus, because
    the winds were contrary.

5   And when we had sailed over the sea of Cilicia and Pamphylia, we came to
    Myra, a city of Lycia.

6   And there the centurion found a ship of Alexandria sailing into Italy; and he
    put us therein.

7   And when we had sailed slowly many days, and scarce were come over
    against Cnidus, the wind not suffering us, we sailed under Crete, over
    against Salmone;

8   And, hardly passing it, came unto a place which is called The fair havens;
    nigh whereunto was the city of Lasea.

9   Now when much time was spent, and when sailing was now dangerous,
    because the fast was now already past.

WISDOM REMAINS IN SAFETY

Luke was pointing out that hardly any wind was blowing, and
they weren't able to make much headway. In addition, winter was
drawing near, when great storms would arise, so it was a particularly
dangerous time to be sailing in the Mediterranean. Luke continues
his account:

ACTS 27:9–12

9   Paul admonished them,

10 And said unto them, Sirs, I perceive that this voyage will be with hurt and
    much damage, not only of the lading and ship, but also of our lives.

11 Nevertheless the centurion believed the master and the owner of the ship,
    more than those things which were spoken by Paul.

12 Because the haven was not commodious to winter in, the more part advised
    to depart thence also, if by any means they might attain to Phenice, and there
    to winter.

This port was not well supplied with accommodations, so they
decided to winter someplace that was better equipped. Sometimes it's
better to stay in the safe place where you are than to seek an unknown
place. I learned this when I was learning to fly.

When the weather was bad, the Director of Flying would ground us young cadets so we wouldn't get hurt. We would always complain, "What's the matter? Don't they think we can fly in this kind of weather? Sure, we can handle it."

DOWN HERE VS. UP THERE

My instructor said to me one day, "Brian, just remember this: It's better for you to be *down here* wishing you were *up there* than to be up there wishing you were down here."

Likewise, when weather is terrible, and you're in a little boat that's bobbing around like a cork, it would be far better to stay in some mediocre port than it would be to go looking for a better one and get caught up in what happened to Paul and his shipmates.

Paul had wisdom, and the centurion who was his guard didn't. Because Paul's wisdom was disregarded, they went through a great trial.

Have you ever been at sea in a small boat when it got rough? Bill, the navigator who flew with me for years, had a sail boat when we were stationed in Southern California, and we would go sailing in it sometimes.

One day we were sailing near Catalina Island and San Clemente, and a great storm came up. As we headed back for Oceanside, that boat was bobbing like a cork. It was a 36-foot sailing sloop, but in those winds, my friend and his helper had all they could do to keep the thing upright. One minute all we could see was water, and the next minute all we could see were clouds.

AT THE MERCY OF A VIOLENT STORM

Bill and I had our sons with us, and they thought it was the greatest experience they had ever had! I've never been so seasick in my life! It was terrible. Your whole body screams at you.

That's what Paul experienced for fourteen days. Can you imagine it? I can't. That little boat was acting like a roller coaster, and the passengers were just along for the ride. Luke describes it for us:

ACTS 27:13–20

13 And when the south wind blew softly, supposing that they had attained their purpose, loosing thence, they sailed close by Crete.

14 But not long after there arose against it a tempestuous wind, called Euroclydon.

15 And when the ship was caught, and could not bear up into the wind, we let her drive.

16 And running under a certain island which is called Clauda, we had much work to come by the boat:

17 Which when they had taken up, they used helps, undergirding the ship; and, fearing lest they should fall into the quicksands, strake [struck] sail, and so were driven.

18 And we being exceedingly tossed with a tempest, the next day they lightened the ship;

19 And the third day we cast out with our own hands the tackling of the ship.

20 And when neither sun nor stars in many days appeared, and no small tempest lay on us, all hope that we should be saved was then taken away.

THE ANGEL OF THE LORD VISITS PAUL

There was no natural hope for them to survive this. They were not even directing that ship anymore; it was just going where the wind blew it and where the sea pushed it. They were just along for the ride. I'm sure they were too seasick to eat anything, as Luke the physician seems to hint in the following:

ACTS 27:21–24

21 But after long abstinence, Paul stood forth in the midst of them, and said, Sirs, ye should have hearkened unto me, and not have loosed from Crete, and to have gained this harm and loss.

22 And now I exhort you to be of good cheer: for there shall be no loss of any man's life among you, but of the ship.

23 *For there stood by me this night the angel of God*, whose I am, and whom I serve,

24 Saying, Fear not, Paul; thou must be brought before Caesar: and, lo, God hath given thee all them that sail with thee.

Why didn't God say that to Paul? Why did He need an angel to say it to him? Because Paul probably couldn't have heard anything at that moment except wretched groans from seasick men all around him—and some of those groans were probably coming from him—after fourteen days in a violent storm.

THE SPIRIT IS AFFECTED BY THE BODY

But Paul had help, didn't he? An angel came and stood by him in those unusual, dangerous circumstances where his body was so affected by what he was experiencing.

Have you ever noticed that when you are not feeling well in your body, your spirit is affected by it? It is more difficult to believe for healing when the body is under a great attack than when it is well.

Why? Because the spirit, the soul, and the body are all connected, and they influence each other. Whenever there is a great negative influence on your flesh, you will need some help spiritually. Paul received this kind of help.

ACTS 27:24–27

24 Fear not, Paul; thou must be brought before Caesar: and, lo, God hath given thee all them that sail with thee.

25 Wherefore, sirs, be of good cheer: for I believe God, that it shall be even as it was told me.

26 Howbeit we must be cast upon a certain island.

27 But when the fourteenth night was come, as we were driven up and down in Adria, about midnight the shipmen deemed that they drew near to some country.

GOD'S WORD COMES TO PASS

They floundered, and the ship broke up, but everyone on board somehow made it safely to the shore, just like God had said through the angel.

They landed on a little island in the middle of the Mediterranean, not even knowing where they were. Landing on solid ground was a form of help, too, wasn't it? Don't you think it was comforting to them to get off that ship? Did they need assistance to make it to the island? Yes, they got everything they needed. The angels of God provided it for them!

Angels contact things in the natural realm to change them for your benefit. They are sent forth to minister for you who shall be heirs of salvation and for you who already are.

7

ANGELS EXECUTE JUDGMENT

Sometimes people get the idea that because God indulges us and allows us a long time to repent, He doesn't mean what He says. But He does mean what He says! Just because He is longsuffering doesn't imply He doesn't mean what He says.

Sometimes sinful practices that need to be corrected have continued over a long period of time. When a person does not repent, eventually God judges that person. Some people think God never judges, but someone is going to judge them for doing wrong.

Who do you want to judge you: God or the devil? I'll take God every time. I won't take man's judgment and I won't take the devil's judgment over God's judgment, because He tempers everything He does with mercy. His tender mercies are over *all* His works, according to Psalm 145:9.

In this chapter we are going to see how angels get involved in executing the judgment of God's Word. This doesn't mean that God has suddenly become only a judge. However, we must always bear in mind that the New Testament says, *"It is a fearful thing to fall into the hands of the living God"* (Heb. 10:31).

This is not something you want to happen to you; but if it comes right down to it, you're a lot better off in His hands than you would be in anyone else's.

"GREAT ARE HIS MERCIES"

As we shall see, King David was given three choices of how God would judge him and the nation of Israel for mistakes he and the nation had made. David said to Gad the prophet, *"I am in a great strait: let me fall now into the hand of the Lord; for very great are his mercies: but let me not fall into the hand of man"* (1 Chron. 21:13).

Therefore, the king's and the nation's judgment for unbelief came from God's hands through the ministry of angels.

Even if God is judging you, *He* is not your problem. Don't get the idea that God is not good. Judgment is not a *bad* thing. When God is involved in it, it's a *good* thing, and it's for the good of the person with whom God is dealing.

We have seen how angels protect and keep you from harm. We have seen how your responsibility is to authorize their actions by your lifestyle and the words you speak from your heart. We have seen how angels help us do the work God has called us to do, and how they are God's messengers sent to minister for us. Now we are going to examine how they execute the judgments of God's Word.

WHEN ANGELS APPEAR

We previously looked at Genesis 18 and 19 to understand how angelic beings appear on earth. Now we will look at these chapters again, but this time we will examine what angels do when they appear.

In Genesis chapter 18, two angels accompanied the angel of the Lord and appeared to Abraham out in the plains of Mamre, and the Lord spoke to Abraham and Sarah about the fact they were going to have a son.

Then the two angels went on their way toward Sodom and Gomorrah, but the Lord remained with Abraham while Abraham made intercession for those wicked cities. Evidently, he also made intercession for Lot, because when destruction came, the Bible says, *"God remembered Abraham, and sent Lot out of the midst of the overthrow"* (Gen. 19:29).

The two angels spent the night safely in Lot's house and asked him early the next morning:

GENESIS 19:12–20

12 Hast thou here any besides? son in law, and thy sons, and thy daughters, and whatsoever thou hast in the city, bring them out of this place:

13 For we will destroy this place, because the cry of them is waxen great before the face of the Lord; and *the Lord hath sent us to destroy it.*

14 Lot went out, and spake unto his sons in law, which married his daughters, and said, Up, get you out of this place; for the Lord will destroy this city. But he seemed as one that mocked unto his sons in law.

15 And when the morning arose, then the angels hastened Lot, saying, Arise, take thy wife, and thy two daughters, which are here; lest thou be consumed in the iniquity of the city.

16 And while he lingered, the men laid hold upon his hand, and upon the hand of his wife, and upon the hand of his two daughters; the Lord being merciful unto him: and they brought him forth, and set him without the city.

17 And then it came to pass, when they had brought them forth abroad, that he said, Escape for thy life; look not behind thee, neither stay thou in all the plain; escape to the mountain, lest thou be consumed.

18 And Lot said unto them, Oh, not so, my Lord:

19 Behold now, thy servant hath found grace in thy sight, and thou hast magnified thy mercy, which thou hast shewed unto me in saving my life; and I cannot escape to the mountain, lest some evil take me, and I die:

20 Behold now, this city is near to flee unto, and it is a little one: Oh, let me escape thither (is it not a little one?) and my soul shall live.

LOT NEEDED WALLS

Lot desperately wanted walls around him! His faith wasn't very well developed. He thought those puny walls would be his security. Even though God was right there talking to him through the angels, he still didn't fully understand God's ability to deliver.

GENESIS 19:21–29

21 And he said unto him, See, I have accepted thee concerning this thing also, that I will not overthrow this city, for the which thou hast spoken.

22 Haste thee, escape thither; for *I cannot do any thing till thou be come thither.* Therefore the name of the city was called Zoar.

23 The sun was risen upon the earth when Lot entered into Zoar.

24 Then the Lord rained upon Sodom and upon Gomorrah brimstone and fire from the Lord out of heaven;

25 And he overthrew those cities, and all the plain, and all the inhabitants of the cities, and that which grew upon the ground.

26 But his wife looked back from behind him, and she became a pillar of salt.

27 And Abraham gat up early in the morning to the place where he stood before the Lord:

28 And he looked toward Sodom and Gomorrah, and toward all the land of the plain, and beheld, and, lo, the smoke of the country went up as the smoke of a furnace.

29 And it came to pass, when God destroyed the cities of the plain, that God remembered Abraham and sent Lot out of the midst of the overthrow, when he overthrew the cities in the which Lot dwelt.

ANGELS WORK FOR THE RIGHTEOUS

You can see from this that angels came to execute that judgment. They said they did. They said God had sent them for that purpose, yet while they were executing judgment on the ungodly, what were they doing for the righteous? They were protecting them from the judgment that fell on the ungodly.

Don't confuse the judgment that comes upon the ungodly because of their hardheartedness and unrepentant hearts with the judgment that comes upon the godly from God. He doesn't mix up these two kinds of judgment.

God deals with people according to what they know, according to what they have done, and according to whether or not they have repented.

Even then, His purpose is for *life*, not *death*. God takes *no* pleasure in the death of the wicked, He insists in Ezekiel 18:23. Does God want to judge the *wicked?* No, He does not. Why does He do it, then? Because if He doesn't, they will affect the righteous more and more in an ungodly way.

And why does He judge the *righteous* when they have been unrepentant and do not obey? We will discuss that next.

JUDGING PRESUMPTUOUS SIN

In First Chronicles chapter 21 we find a case of God judging the righteous, His people Israel, and again angels are involved in judgment.

1 CHRONICLES 21:1–2

1   And Satan stood up against Israel, and provoked David to number Israel.

2   And David said to Joab and to the rulers of the people, Go, number Israel from Beer-sheba even to Dan; and bring the number of them to me, that I may know it.

Notice that Satan had tempted David, and David fell victim to that temptation. He did something he knew was wrong. When you sin knowingly, and you know you are sinning, that's called "presumptuous sin," because how do you know that the grace of God is going to be there for you?

How do you know that you are going to be able to receive the grace of God to forgive you for that sin if you don't know the grace of God can keep you from sinning?

After you have sinned presumptuously, are you sure you will have *faith* to receive forgiveness for what you did? After all, you didn't believe God was able to keep you from sinning. Think about it! Sin is a barrier between you and God, and sin is always against God.

YOUR SIN AFFECTS OTHERS

Furthermore, presumptuous sin always affects more than one person. Jonah sinned presumptuously when he ran away from the direction God had given him. And who was affected by his sin—only Jonah? Everyone on that ship was affected by it.

You say, "How? They were innocent." Maybe they weren't involved in Jonah's sin, but they were affected by the judgment that came upon him for it.

If you want to spend three days and three nights in the belly of a whale, go ahead: Sin presumptuously. But it isn't even halfway smart to sin when you *know* you're sinning, because all believers ought to know by now that presumptuous sin will bring worse judgment on you than it would if you were ignorant.

THE DANGER OF PRESUMPTUOUS SIN

Ignorance is easily overcome by knowledge. Presumption is a different process. I will not tell you that you *can't* be forgiven for presumptuous sin, but it is a dangerous practice, because if you *keep* sinning presumptuously, someday you won't repent!

If you know the dangers of presumptuous sin, why would you want to go in that direction where you could get so hard in your heart that you wouldn't even repent when God spoke to you? It would be rather stupid to go in that direction, knowing what is down there.

If you walk down a road in pitch-black darkness and come to a sign that says "Bridge Out Ahead," are you going to keep walking in that direction? Why not? Because sooner or later you are going to fall into the river or chasm that the bridge no longer spans.

The same kind of principle applies spiritually. If you go along presuming that you can sin and get away with it somehow and supposedly "repent" the next day, I don't think that is really repentance at all. Sooner or later you are going to fall into that chasm. Don't walk presumptuously toward sin.

JOAB SUDDENLY TURNS SPIRITUAL

Joab was David's army commander and his cousin. If you read about Joab in other places, you will find he wasn't the most spiritual person in Israel. In fact, he was one of the *least* spiritual! He was a murderer. He murdered two other men whom he thought might take his job.

1 CHRONICLES 21:3

3   And Joab answered, The Lord make his people an hundred times so many more as they be: but, my lord the king, are they not all my lord's servants? why then doth my lord require this thing? why will he be a cause of trespass to Israel?

David was the king of the nation, but even Joab knew if he went out and did what David had told him to do and numbered all the people, it would bring judgment not only upon David, but upon all Israel!

Do you think David didn't know it? He knew it, all right.

1 CHRONICLES 21:4–5

4 Nevertheless the king's word prevailed against Joab. Wherefore Joab departed, and went throughout all Israel, and came to Jerusalem.

5 And Joab gave the sum of the number of the people unto David. And all they of Israel were a thousand thousand and an hundred thousand men that drew sword: and Judah was four hundred threescore and ten thousand men that drew sword.

That's a lot of men. That's 1,100,000 men in the whole army, 400,000 of them in Judah.

JOAB QUITS!

1 CHRONICLES 21:6

6 But Levi and Benjamin counted he not among them: for the king's word was abominable to Joab.

Even before he completed his census job, Joab quit, because it was such an abomination to him; furthermore, he knew judgment was coming to King David and Israel because of it.

1 CHRONICLES 21:7

7 And God was displeased with this thing; therefore *he smote Israel.*

Who smote Israel? It doesn't say the devil did.

1 CHRONICLES 21:8

8 And David said unto God, I have sinned greatly, because I have done this thing: but now, I beseech thee, do away the iniquity of thy servant; for I have done very foolishly.

It's absolute foolishness to commit presumptuous sin, and it has an effect on other people, not just on you; especially when you are in a position of leadership.

DAVID'S THREE CHOICES

1 CHRONICLES 21:9–10

9 And the Lord spake unto Gad, David's seer, saying,

10 Go and tell David, saying, Thus saith the Lord, I offer thee three things.

A seer is a prophet, and God spoke to this prophet of God. The phrase *"Thus saith the Lord"* meant God was speaking.

1 CHRONICLES 21:10–12

10 I offer thee three things: choose thee one of them, that I may do it unto thee.

11 So Gad came to David, and said unto him, Thus saith the Lord, Choose thee

12 Either three years' famine; or three months to be destroyed before thy foes, while that the sword of thine enemies overtaketh thee; or else three days the sword of the Lord, even the pestilence, in the land, *and the angel of the Lord destroying* throughout all the coasts of Israel.

DON'T BLAME THE DEVIL FOR EVERYTHING

It doesn't say the devil would be destroying throughout all the coasts of Israel, does it? The prophet said the angel of the Lord would be destroying.

I have heard faith teachers say, "God never did such a thing." But if that is true, the Word of God doesn't mean what it says. And if it doesn't mean what it says, how do you know that First Peter 2:24— *"By whose stripes ye were healed"*—means what it says?

It's time to grow up and recognize that God is involved in judgment as well as in blessing. And I am glad He is. I am glad the devil doesn't do all of this, because you wouldn't have any mercy at all if he did.

It's too bad that our sin ever gets to the point where God has to intervene. In the case of believers, it should never go that far. We ought to be judging ourselves, as Paul wrote in First Corinthians 11:31–32, and not be judged as the world is.

SOWING AND REAPING

In the New Testament, God said to all believers:

GALATIANS 6:7–8

7 Be not deceived; God is not mocked: for whatsoever a man *soweth*, that shall he also *reap.*

8 For he that soweth to his flesh shall of the *flesh* reap *corruption;* but he that soweth to the Spirit shall of the Spirit reap *life everlasting.*

If we sow to the flesh, we will of the flesh reap corruption. God sees to it that His Word comes to pass. It is He Who sees to it that it comes to pass in the way of blessing, protection, deliverance, and so forth as well as in judgment.

Who do you think it is who sees to it that judgment also comes? It's God, not the devil. He doesn't call up the devil and say, "Now, devil, I've turned this one over to you for the destruction of the flesh. See to it that it gets done."

The devil wouldn't do it. If he knew what the will of God was and what God wanted done, he wouldn't do it. Do you think he's reliable? Do you think God can depend on him, telling him to do something and knowing he's going to do it?

No, but God does know what the devil will do, and He uses that foreknowledge to turn a person over to Satan for the destruction of the flesh.

God doesn't give the devil his marching orders every morning, and he doesn't give him directions as how to do it. God does it by His foreknowledge. He knows what the devil will do before he does it. Therefore, God can turn a person over to him for the destruction of his or her flesh.

THE DESTRUCTION OF THE FLESH

The Apostle Paul, writing in First Corinthians 5:3–5, instructs the Corinthian church and its leadership *"To deliver such an one unto Satan for the destruction of the flesh, that the spirit may be saved in the day of the Lord Jesus"* (v. 5). In this case, the man was living in an immoral relationship with his father's wife (v. 1).

Living unrepentant in fornication (sin) will lead to greater problems if that person does not repent. Stronger measures here called for delivering the man to Satan for the destruction of that fleshly unrepentant attitude and its action.

How do we do such a thing? Being led by the Lord, we put such a person out of fellowship (vv. 9–13). Also led by God, we stop interceding or making supplication for that person.

If he tastes the fruit of his own way—bitter fruit and hard consequences—he may then repent and turn away from his sin, confess it to God, and receive grace to overcome it. That is exactly what happened in this case, as we read in Second Corinthians 2:5–10.

2 CORINTHIANS 2:5-10

5 But if any have caused grief, he hath not grieved me, but in part: that I may not overcharge you all.

6 Sufficient to such a man is this punishment, which was inflicted of many.

7 So that contrariwise ye ought rather to forgive him, and comfort him, lest perhaps such a one should be swallowed up with overmuch sorrow.

8 Wherefore I beseech you that ye would confirm your love toward him.

9 For to this end also did I write, that I might know the proof of you, whether ye be obedient in all things.

10 To whom ye forgive any thing, I forgive also: for if I forgave any thing, to whom I forgave it, for your sakes forgave I it in the person of Christ.

DAVID'S CHOICE

David chose pestilence in the land. This pestilence did not come from Heaven, because there is no pestilence in Heaven. Where did it come from? Right here on the earth.

You will be in contact with pestilence in many places you go today, but you won't get it. Why not? Because God is protecting you from it. All He would really have to do is withdraw His hand of protection, and you would get some form of pestilence.

Pestilence is a form of virulent disease. It is fast spreading and very deadly. There are several kinds of it, but you are protected from it day by day.

If you ask a doctor what kinds of germs or viruses are in your body, he or she would tell you there are germs right now in every one of you that could give you tuberculosis, for example, yet you don't get it. Why? Because God is protecting you from it.

FALLING INTO THE HAND OF GOD

The prophet listed David's three choices—famine, military defeat, or pestilence—and added, *"Now therefore advise thyself what word I shall bring again to him that sent me"* (1 Chron. 21:12).

1 CHRONICLES 21:13

13 And David said unto Gad, I am in a great strait let me fall now into the hand of the Lord; for very great are his mercies: but let me not fall into the hand of man.

God will not judge anyone without His tender mercies tempering that judgment.

1 CHRONICLES 21:14

14 So the Lord sent pestilence upon Israel: and there fell of Israel seventy thousand men.

Again, the Lord didn't send pestilence from Heaven. It didn't come from His hand. He hasn't got it, and He can't give it. But it is here on earth, and He does protect you from it. The loss of 70,000 men was not a small thing.

1 CHRONICLES 21:15

15 And God sent an angel unto Jerusalem to destroy it and as he was destroying, the Lord beheld, and he repented him of the evil.

Does this mean God repented of some bad thing He had done? No, God has never done wrong. Anything you ever see Him doing in the Bible is right. He cannot do wrong. He is just and right, and His tender mercies are over all His works, including this one. If God ever did wrong, that would be the end of everything! The evil that God changed the direction of was further unnecessary destruction of human life from the pestilence.

"IT IS ENOUGH!"

"It is enough!" God said to the angel who was destroying, changing the course of the action, because the judgment had fulfilled its purpose.

If God had not judged Israel, the people would have kept going in the sinful direction of the heathen nations around them, and they would have become just like those peoples.

In fact, at one point when they had backslidden, God said to them, *"You're even worse than the people around you, because you have denied the knowledge you have to become like they are"* (Hosea 4:16–17; 5:9–12 NASB).

Thus, God will judge His people to keep that from happening. That is the only way He can turn things around when they will not listen to Him.

When people sin presumptuously, they are not listening to God. Your conscience will not allow you to sin without first warning you, and if you are listening to God when He speaks to you, you won't sin presumptuously.

WHEN YOU BLUNDER

If you just blunder along and do something sinful, not hearing what God said to you, He will forgive you, cleanse you from that unrighteousness, and restore you to fellowship with Him.

However, if you have been warned, but you go ahead and sin anyway, you will be judged, and you won't like the consequences any more than David liked the consequences he reaped with his sin. The story resumes with verse 15, where God says to the destroying angel:

1 CHRONICLES 21:15–19, 26–30

15 It is enough, stay now thine hand. And the angel of the Lord stood by the threshingfloor of Ornan the Jebusite.

16 *And David lifted up his eyes, and saw the angel of the Lord* stand between the earth and the heaven, having a drawn sword in his hand stretched out over Jerusalem. Then David and the elders of Israel, who were clothed in sackcloth, fell upon their faces.

17 And David said unto God, Is it not I that commanded the people to be numbered? even I it is that have sinned and done evil indeed; but as for these sheep, what have they done? let thine hand, I pray thee, O Lord my God, be on me, and on my father's house; but not on thy people, that they should be plagued.

18 Then the angel of the Lord commanded Gad to say to David, that David should go up, and set up an altar unto the Lord in the threshingfloor of Ornan the Jebusite.

19 And David went up at the saying of Gad.

26 And David built there an altar unto the Lord, and offered burnt offerings and peace offerings, and called upon the Lord; and he answered him from heaven by fire upon the altar of burnt offering.

27 And the Lord commanded the angel; and he put up his sword again into the sheath thereof.

28 At that time when David saw that the Lord had answered him in the threshingfloor of Ornan the Jebusite, then he sacrificed there.

29 For the tabernacle of the Lord, which Moses made in the wilderness, and the altar of the burnt offering, were at that season in the high place at Gibeon.

30 But David could not go before it to inquire of God: for he was afraid because of the sword of the angel of the Lord.

When Judgment Ends in Repentance

You can see from this passage that God did judge until the net result was repentance. And when His judgment ended in repentance, the judgment ceased.

God's judgment is not something you should be depressed about. You ought to be glad and thankful for it, because God is wiser than any man. He knows what is necessary.

If it was necessary for Him to bring judgment in Old Testament times in order to bring forth Christ in the earth, and if judgment is necessary in this age to bring forth Christ's likeness in the Body of Christ, then judgment is a good thing, not a bad thing. And remember, it is always tempered with mercy.

Angels Execute the Judgment of God

Angels, as we have seen, are involved in executing the judgment of God. We find another example of this in Second Kings chapter 19. In this case, God's judgment fell upon unbelieving people who were trying to keep God's covenant people from receiving His covenant promise.

Sennacherib, the Assyrian king, and his huge army invaded Judah. He, his army commander, and others taunted King Hezekiah, saying it wouldn't make any difference if the Jews went into the Temple of God and prayed for deliverance, because their God couldn't save them from the Assyrian forces.

The Assyrian commander bragged that the gods of other nations hadn't been able to save them when the Assyrians invaded their lands, and the Jews' God wouldn't be able to save them, either.

But God had promised the Jews that whenever sword or peril came upon them, if they went into the Temple and stood before Him and called upon Him with all their hearts, He would deliver them. And that's what they did in this case.

They went into the Temple and told God they were depending on Him for their deliverance, and the prophet Isaiah stood on the wall of Jerusalem and spoke the Word over the situation.

Sennacherib had put himself in the position of saying, "There is no way your God can deliver you from me." But there was a way, and the truth was, God *could* deliver His covenant people who were believing Him from the Assyrian king and his army.

THE PROPHET'S MESSAGE

Isaiah prophesied this before night fell:

2 KINGS 19:32–35

32 Therefore thus saith the Lord concerning the king of Assyria, He shall not come into this city, nor shoot an arrow there, nor come before it with shield, nor cast a bank against it.

33 By the way that he came, by the same shall he return, and shall not come into this city, saith the Lord.

34 *For I will defend this city, to save it, for mine own sake, and for my servant David's sake.*

35 And it came to pass that night, that *the angel of the Lord went out, and smote* in the camp of the Assyrians an hundred fourscore and five thousand.

THE KING'S MISTAKE

The angel of the Lord went out against the Assyrians, and 185,000 soldiers died in their camp because their king, who had surrounded Jerusalem with his soldiers, said, "God can't keep His Word to deliver His covenant people."

Who is going to find out differently? Who has to give in? The one who was trying to keep God from keeping His Word: the Assyrian king. Of course, God wasn't going around looking for Assyrians to kill. He didn't want to kill any Assyrians.

Why, then, did He do it? Because they were standing in the way of His keeping His promise to Israel. The Assyrians had stood before the wall of Jerusalem and challenged God, "You can't deliver the Jews, and we're going to show you that You can't." They found out that God could and would keep His promise to His people.

God had to judge the Assyrians. He does what He has to do, but He doesn't do any more than He has to. He takes no pleasure in the death of the wicked. He was grieved because it was necessary for those soldiers to lose their lives, but He will keep His word for those who believe it.

SENNACHERIB SLINKS AWAY

2 KINGS 19:35–36

35 When they arose early in the morning, behold, they were all dead corpses.

36 So Sennacherib king of Assyria departed, and went and returned, and dwelt at Nineveh.

When he saw what happened, King Sennacherib got out of there in a hurry! You might say he put his tail between his legs and ran. But Sennacherib's story does not end here. His life did not turn out well.

2 KINGS 19:37

37 And it came to pass, as he was worshipping in the house of Nisroch his god, that Adrammelech and Sharezer his own sons smote him with the sword: and they escaped into the land of Armenia, And Esarhaddon his son reigned in his stead.

History books are full of King Sennacherib's military exploits in many nations, but most don't say one word about the defeat he suffered in Judah at God's hands. This shows you who is in charge of writing history!

The devil doesn't care if you write accounts of secular history, but whenever history tells of God triumphing over the devil, he makes sure that information doesn't get into the history books.

ANGELS IN THE GREAT TRIBULATION

In Revelation 8:2, let's look at the role angels of God will play in administering judgment in the time of the Great Tribulation.

REVELATION 8:2, 6
2   And I saw the seven angels which stood before God; and to them were given seven trumpets.
6   And the seven angels which had the seven trumpets prepared themselves to sound.

These are godly angelic beings. As you read further, you will find that great judgment comes upon unbelieving, unrepentant, backslidden mankind as well as people who have gone well past the point where God can still reach them. Angels will execute judgment on such people in the time of Great Tribulation.

Revelation 9:20–21 tells what kinds of people will be afflicted by these plagues.

REVELATION 9:20–21
20 And the rest of the men which were not killed by these plagues yet repented *not of the works of their hands,* that they should not *worship devils, and idols of gold,* and silver, and brass, and stone, and of wood: which neither can see, nor hear, nor walk:
21 Neither repented they of their murders, nor of their *sorceries,* nor of their *fornication,* nor of their *thefts.*

DESTROYING THE WORLD SYSTEM

In chapter 16, you will find that angels will also be involved when the wrath of God is poured out to utterly destroy the world system.

REVELATION 16:1–4

1 And I heard a great voice out of the temple saying to the seven angels, Go your ways, and pour out the vials of the wrath of God upon the earth.

2 And the first went, and poured out his vial upon the earth; and there fell a noisome and grievous sore upon the men which had the mark of the beast, and upon them which worshipped his image.

3 And the second angel poured out his vial upon the sea; and it became as the blood of a dead man: and every living soul died in the sea.

4 And the third angel poured out his vial upon the rivers and fountains of waters; and they became blood.

The angels of God will be involved in executing all these judgments. Even when the wrath of God comes, they will be involved in it. So they execute the judgments of God's Word.

ANGELIC CORRECTION

Something that godly angels always do is to correct any person who attempts to worship them. In Hebrews 1:6 we read: *"When he* [God] *bringeth in the firstbegotten into the world, he saith, And let all the angels of God worship him."*

Angels of God worship only Jesus, the Son of man, the God man. They will not allow any human being to worship them.

Why are we human beings so apt to worship angels? Because when they appear in all their glory, they are such awesome beings, we might confuse an angel with the Lord Himself. However, angels won't allow us to worship them. They are always very clear on that point.

ANGELS THAT DIRECT WORSHIP

The fourth chapter of Revelation describes the function of the four living creatures, who are angelic beings. The *King James Version* terms them "beasts," but the Greek word is *zoon*, which comes from the Greek word *zoe*, which means "life." So these are living creatures, and most modern translations of the Bible call them that.

These four living creatures live in the presence of God. Revelation 4:8–11 describes them and their duties.

REVELATION 4:8-11

8 And the four beasts had each of them six wings about him; and they were full of eyes within: and they rest not day and night, saying, Holy, holy, holy, Lord God Almighty, which was, and is, and is to come.

9 And when those living beasts give glory and honour and thanks to him that sat on the throne, who liveth for ever and ever,

10 The four and twenty elders fall down before him that sat on the throne, and worship him that liveth for ever and ever, and cast their crowns before the throne, saying,

11 Thou art worthy, O Lord, to receive glory and honour and power: for thou hast created all things, and for thy pleasure they are and were created.

"Holy, holy, holy, Lord God Almighty, which was and is, and is to come." The four living creatures proclaim that constantly in the presence of God. When they do, they direct men who are already in Heaven—the 24 elders who represent the redeemed from all the ages who are presently in Heaven—to worship God. And if we are spiritually minded, they can do the same for us.

We know that when we are worshipping God, the angels of God are worshipping with us. Whether or not you perceive them with your senses at the moment (and most of the time we don't), they still are present.

JOHN'S MISTAKE IN HEAVEN

Looking further into this Book of Revelation, in chapter 19 we discover an experience John had. Was John a mature saint when he was caught away to Heaven in the Book of Revelation? Yes, he was. He had the ability to judge between what was correct or incorrect.

But even John, a mature saint who was standing in Heaven and seeing things that are simply not describable in human language, did something that was not acceptable. (Of course, he did not do it presumptuously or to offend anyone.) Read in verse 10 what happened after he had been instructed by an angel:

REVELATION 19:10
10 And I fell at his feet to worship him. And he said unto me, See thou do it
   not.

The angel would not permit it. He wouldn't even allow John to begin to worship him. Authentic angels of God won't allow it; however, fallen spirits, appearing as angels of light, will accept worship from human beings. That is one way you can tell them apart.

The angel John sought to worship told him further:

REVELATION 19:10
10 I am thy fellow servant, and of thy brethren that have the testimony of Jesus:
   worship God: for the testimony of Jesus is the spirit of prophecy.

AN "ANGEL" NAMED MORONI

There is a cult called Mormonism which was founded because a supposed "angel" appeared to a Christian man and told him that he had revelation that was *beyond* the Bible.

Thus, the *Book of Mormon* originated from a fallen angel who revealed its contents to Joseph Smith. Smith didn't know enough about the Bible to recognize that this "revelation" was in error, so he received it.

Now the cult of Mormonism sends many missionaries around the world to make converts. The name of the "angel" that appeared to Smith was Moroni. That's "moron" with an *I* added to it. Sometimes I think even the devil has a sense of humor!

If you listen to some angel that gives you revelation *beyond* the Bible, you're in the same category! It's moronic to listen to any voice that would tell you anything that's *beyond* the Word of God, regardless how it appears or wherever you think it is coming from.

DON'T GO BEYOND THE WORD OF GOD

Don't listen to a word of anything that is said to be *beyond* the Word of God. Rebuke it because *there is no revelation beyond the Word of God.* There is nothing that can be added to the Word.

Paul clearly warns about this error in Galatians 1:8: *"But though we, or an angel from heaven, preach any other gospel unto you than that which we have preached unto you, let him be accursed."*

The Holy Spirit may give you personal direction that is not found on the pages of the Bible, but His direction will always be in *agreement* with everything that is in the Bible.

In chapter 22, John heard and saw more. There he was, caught away in Heaven, receiving this revelation that has been communicated to us, and Jesus said to him:

REVELATION 22:7–8

7 Behold, I come quickly: blessed is he that keepeth the sayings of the prophecy of this book.

8 And I John saw these things, and heard them. And when I had heard and seen, I fell down to worship before the feet of the angel which shewed me these things.

What was John doing? Was he worshipping the angel? Since he had already been corrected the first time, I think he was simply falling down to worship Jesus, Who had spoken and spoke again, thus indicating His presence.

When John fell at the angel's feet in chapter 19, he was immediately corrected. Here in chapter 22, the angel wouldn't let him do anything that even appeared like he was worshipping an angel.

The Bible says we are supposed to avoid even the *appearance* of evil. So an angel of God, being zealous as he is for the One he serves, will never allow even the appearance of angel worship to happen.

Angels always direct human beings' worship to Jesus Christ. As we saw in Hebrews 1:6, the Father commanded angels to worship Jesus when He came into the world. Like the angels, we, too, must always direct our worship toward the Son of God.

8

Agents of God's Government on Earth

In this chapter, we will learn how angels are the agents of God's government in the earth. We will examine ways angels touch the world around us to accomplish the will of God.

All our efforts should always be directed toward that purpose. We are not here simply to do our own will. We are not on earth to do our programs or effect only our desires.

Jesus prayed and sweat great drops of blood in the Garden of Gethsemane that He would not do anything except His Father's will. There was nothing tainted about Jesus' will.

Jesus did not need to get His mind renewed like we do, because He had a renewed mind. Furthermore, His soul was not becoming saved, because it was saved. And His flesh was not like ours. God was His Father, and there was nothing at all in Him that was wrong or evil.

He prayed, *"Nevertheless not my will, but thine, be done"* (Luke 22:42).

Sometimes when we look at our government, we think, "Woe is us. Will our leaders ever learn? Will they ever improve in certain areas?" However, if you and I were not praying for the government, imagine how bad conditions would be.

Can God accomplish His purpose through a human form of government that is faulty? Yes. If you will pray, He can, but He must influence those leaders somehow. Angels get involved in this process. They have been involved in influencing leaders throughout the ages, and they are still involved in it when we pray for our government.

Do you remember that Daniel prayed for those who were in authority? He prayed for Nebuchadnezzar all the time, even though Nebuchadnezzar was a man full of rage and fury who was firing up his furnace to incinerate Hebrews!

Notice Daniel didn't go out in the streets and campaign against the godless king; he prayed for him. That should give us a clue as to what *we* ought to be doing in our age.

When we are praying about governmental matters, Jesus' words *"Thy will be done"* are a good admonition for us to bear in mind. Most of us have political preferences and affiliations. I used to have one, but I no longer cling to it. I found I can't pray with authority like I'm supposed to pray when I have a certain political "agenda."

It's a good thing to remember that God's will is what we are after; not our own and not someone else's. We are after the will of God, period. That is what we are to pray about.

"HIS KINGDOM RULETH OVER ALL"

Although we have looked at Psalm 103 several times before, there are still things we can learn from it.

PSALM 103:1–2
1   Bless the Lord, O my soul: and all that is within me, bless his holy name.
2   Bless the Lord, O my soul, and forget not all his benefits.

Then the passage goes on to list the benefits before coming to verse 19: *"The Lord hath prepared his throne in the heavens; and his kingdom ruleth over all."*

That is a flat statement. God's kingdom—the kingdom of heaven—rules over other kingdoms! It is in the highest place, far above all other kingdoms.

Of course, that does not mean that God controls everything that happens in all the other kingdoms. He does not, because He has given mankind dominion in the earth. He has also given mankind the power to choose whether or not to serve Him. Every spirit being He ever created was given the power to choose, and He doesn't violate their right. However, He will accomplish His will if we will follow His way.

It is said of Moses and the children of Israel, *"He made known his ways unto Moses, his acts unto the children of Israel"* (Ps. 103:7).

Moses saw more than just the acts and the power of God; he saw His ways. He saw God's *character*. He recognized God's ways of doing things were different from man's ways.

PRAYING FOR THE WILL OF GOD

Therefore, we should not use what we know about our dominion on earth and pray for man's ways to be successful. Instead, we should pray for the will of God to be successful, because His kingdom rules over all. His throne is far above every other throne, dominion, principality, power, might, or anything that is known. The passage continues in verse 20:

PSALM 103:20–21
20 Bless the Lord, ye his angels, that excel in strength, that do his commandments, hearkening unto the voice of his word.
21 Bless ye the Lord, all ye his hosts.

The word "hosts" there is the Hebrew word *sava*. From it we get the compound name Jehovah Sabaoth, which means "the Lord of hosts." He is the Lord of the heavenly hosts.

PSALM 103:21–22
21 Bless ye the Lord, all ye his hosts; ye ministers of his, that do his pleasure.
22 Bless the Lord, all his works in all places of his dominion: bless the Lord, O my soul.

When did God get *dominion* in your life? When you gave it to Him. Did He take it from you before that? Did He come and rip it out of you? Did He take your will away and make you a robot, instructing you, "Stand up. I'll tell you what to do"? No, He didn't do that. He came and took dominion in you when you *gave* it to Him. And that is the way He is going to work in our lives and through our believing for the realm of government on earth.

To summarize, everything that happens in the realm of government isn't God's doing. However, if we will pray as we ought, the things that happen in the realm of government will work toward accomplishing the will of God on earth.

SPIRITUAL WARFARE

In the tenth chapter of Daniel, Daniel had a vision. An angel of God came and revealed that spiritual wickedness in high places had restrained him from coming to Daniel's aid. He said in verse 13: *"The prince of the kingdom of Persia withstood me one and twenty days: but, lo, Michael, one of the chief princes, came to help me; and I remained there with the kings* [or other princes] *of Persia."*

The godly angels did battle with fallen angels in the spirit realm until the evil resistance was overcome. And Daniel's prayer was instrumental in their victory! Later, in verse 20, the angel continued his report: *"Knowest thou wherefore I come unto thee? and now will I return to fight with the prince of Persia: and when I am gone forth, lo, the prince of Grecia shall come."*

The angel explains that when the prince of Persia has been vanquished, another will take his place, and that one will be called the prince of Greece.

AGENTS OF GOD'S GOVERNMENT ON EARTH

Who is talking here? The angel that was speaking to Michael. More than likely, it was Gabriel. It doesn't say so in that chapter, but if you read the surrounding chapters, you can see that it probably was Gabriel.

The story continues into chapter 11, because chapter and verse divisions were added later. Even though the translators didn't always divide chapters where it makes sense, we can still be grateful that they provided us with a good reference help.

This is one of those chapter divisions that doesn't make sense, because the translators cut the angel off right in the middle of what he was saying to Daniel and made a chapter division there:

DANIEL 10:21

21 But I will shew thee that which is noted in the scripture of truth: and there
   is none that holdeth with me in these things, but Michael your prince.

DANIEL 11:1

1 Also I in the first year of Darius the Mede, even I, stood to confirm and to strengthen him.

As we saw, Daniel was a man who prayed for those in authority; especially men like Nebuchadnezzar. And he didn't pray against the king; Daniel prayed *for* the king.

EAST GERMANS TESTIFY

In 1990, we had a *Winter Bible Seminar* at Rhema Bible Training College in Tulsa. Five ministers from East Germany attended. The Berlin Wall had just come down, and that was the first year they could freely leave their country to travel abroad.

These pastors came to hear Brother Kenneth E. Hagin teach, because his teachings had infiltrated through the Iron Curtain before it came down. Also, some of his books had been translated into their own language, and now they wanted to hear more.

When they were invited to the platform, this was the testimony of their spokesman. He said, "For years and years we were Christians. The five of us here were in contact with each other. Most of the country was made up of Communists, so we Christians were rare in the whole population. We pastored a few people, but not many. We stayed in contact with each other because we had our faith in Christ in common."

He continued, "The Communist regime was brutal. People were being killed. The regime affected us negatively all the time, and we prayed *against* it. For years and years we prayed that it would fall, and we prayed that the Communists who were responsible for the killings and repression would get their just rewards. But nothing ever changed; it just got worse."

In the flesh, like these people, we would naturally like to get rid of our enemies. We would like to pray, "God, slay them! Let fire fall on them or something. Remove them!"

The German pastor said, "When we prayed that way, nothing happened. Things just got worse. But we got hold of some teachings by a man named Kenneth E. Hagin. He said that our place as Christians was to pray for kings and those in authority, so we began to pray for Erich Honecker, the leader of the East German Communist party. Within one year of our beginning to pray for him, the Berlin Wall fell, and Honecker was no longer in office."

Political Prayers

Does that tell you anything? You might have your own political agenda, but don't pray along the lines of your political agenda. Pray the way God tells you to pray. God isn't a Republican. The Republicans would like you to think He is, but He isn't. He doesn't care anything about either the Republican or the Democratic platforms.

I'm so naturally conservative, I "clank" when I walk. I was reared that way, but I am learning to become more liberal. Why? Because God wants to change what needs to be changed, and He will change it if we will get in agreement with Him about how it is to be done. However, He also wants to keep what is good. This means I am now a liberal conservative or a conservative liberal, whatever you want to call it.

I don't like labels. I don't want to label myself one thing or another. I want to be free to do what the Word of God says without being hindered by my own thinking or political viewpoint about what is right or wrong.

Man's Idea of Good

Often, man's idea of good is not God's idea of good. When the fruit of the tree of the knowledge of good and evil was eaten in the Garden of Eden, what do you suppose that knowledge really was?

Was the good in that symbolic tree the knowledge of God? No, they already had that knowledge. They were in fellowship with God. They had open communication with God. They knew the goodness of God.

What "good" did they discover when they partook of that tree? *Man's idea of what is good.*

What man thinks is good is a counterfeit of what God says is good. *Man's idea of goodness isn't good at all!* You can go around doing 50 good things a day, but it won't earn you a reward in God's sight, because that's not God's idea of good.

Man has many ideas of what "good" is that are not in agreement with the Word of God. The *motivation* of why you do something makes the difference.

ANOTHER HEATHEN KING

The angel told Daniel, *"Also I in the first year of Darius the Mede, even I, stood to confirm and to strengthen him"* (Dan. 11:1). Who was Darius the Mede? He was the Persian king who took the kingdom away from Nebuchadnezzar's grandson, Belshazzar.

Belshazzar held a famous feast one night; and you remember the dramatic thing that happened: A hand appeared and wrote on the wall, *"Mene, Mene, Tekel, Upharsin."*

The translation Daniel gave the king was, "You have been weighed in the balance and are found wanting, and the kingdom has been removed from you this night."

That very night, the Persians were able to slip past the famed city's defenses, take the kingdom away from Belshazzar, and kill him (Dan. 5:30). Thus, Darius the Mede took the throne of the Babylonians and incorporated the Babylonian Empire into his own empire.

Was Darius a good man? No, he was just another heathen king Daniel had to pray for, continuing all the way to Cyrus the Persian, who finally ended the Jews' Babylonian captivity and released them.

DANIEL DISCOVERS GOD'S WILL

In the ninth chapter of Daniel, we learn that Daniel had discovered in the writings of Jeremiah that the will of God was for the Hebrews in Babylonian captivity to be released after 70 years. It's right here in the ninth chapter:

DANIEL 9:1-6

1 In the first year of Darius the son of Ahasuerus, of the seed of the Medes, which was made king over the realm of the Chaldeans;

2 In the first year of his reign I Daniel understood by books [the book of Jeremiah] the number of the years, where of the word of the Lord came to Jeremiah the prophet, that he would accomplish seventy years in the desolations of Jerusalem.

3 And I set my face unto the Lord God, to seek by prayer and supplications, with fasting, and sackcloth, and ashes:

4 And I prayed unto the Lord my God, and made my confession, and said, O Lord, the great and dreadful God, keeping the covenant and mercy to them that love him, and to them that keep his commandments;

5 We have sinned, and have committed iniquity, and have done wickedly, and have rebelled, even by departing from thy precepts and from thy judgments:

6 Neither have we hearkened unto thy servants the prophets, which spake in thy name to our kings, our princes, and our fathers, and to all the people of the land.

BRINGING THE WILL OF GOD TO PASS

Daniel went on to describe what had happened to the Hebrews because of their transgression of the Law: They were led away to Babylonian captivity. But when Daniel discovered that the will of God was for them to be released from that captivity in 70 years' time, *he set his face to seek God and to bring to pass what he had read in Jeremiah.* Daniel prayed for the will of God to be done! It isn't automatic. Someone on earth needs to pray for it to be done.

Who has dominion in the earth? We Christians do. Therefore, when we pray for the will of God to be done in the earth, it will be done. Why hasn't God's will been done more often in history? Because we haven't prayed like we should have!

Notice Daniel did not write a book entitled *70 Reasons Why We Are Getting Out of Babylon in 70 Years.* He didn't try to capitalize on his knowledge. He didn't go out into the streets and tell everyone about it.

Frequently, that's the fleshly reaction many people have when they think they understand future events. They try to make themselves into an important "somebody" because they think they know something no one else knows. (Although they think they do, they usually don't.)

Daniel didn't do that at all. The Bible doesn't say he started holding special meetings to teach all the Hebrews that their captivity was going to end in 70 years. I'm sure he did bless the people who were around him because of the kind of man he was—a man who wanted to see the will of God done.

Daniel prayed for all those heathen kings. And he didn't pray that they would drop dead; he prayed that they would be successful!

Daniel prayed for 70 years for a succession of heathen kings before the Jews were released. If you are fully persuaded of what the will of God is, you will be patient for 70 years before it comes to pass. But you will also do what you are supposed to do during that period of time to see that it comes to pass.

We believers do have a powerful authority in the earth, but it is to accomplish the will of God; not our own agendas. It is to accomplish what God put us here to accomplish: *We are to preach the Gospel to every nation!*

Therefore, the first and foremost purpose of any kind of prayer like this is that it will facilitate the Church today on earth in preaching the Gospel.

God is not interested in raising up one government and putting down another; He is interested in evangelizing the whole earth. So when we pray, it should be toward that purpose.

ANGELIC HELP IN ANSWERING PRAYER

In the eleventh chapter, the angel said he stood up to confirm and strengthen the heathen king because Daniel was praying for that king!

The angel said he would strengthen that man, confirm his dominion, and direct his actions as king to the extent that he would bring the will of God to pass. The will of God was for Israel to be released out of that kingdom of Babylon—and that is what Daniel was praying toward.

The angel went on to tell how many more kings there would be in Persia—three more, and the fourth would be richer than the rest. He also outlined the things that would happen in that kingdom through succeeding generations.

Today, God's will is still for believers to pray for those in authority, as we see from the following important passage in the New Testament:

1 TIMOTHY 2:1–4

1 I exhort therefore, that, first of all, supplications, prayers, intercessions, and giving of thanks, be made for all men;

2 For kings, and for all that are in authority; that we may lead a quiet and peaceable life in all godliness and honesty.

3 For this is good and acceptable in the sight of God our Saviour;

4 Who will have all men to be saved, and to come unto the knowledge of the truth.

A COMMANDMENT FROM GOD TO PRAY

Just as the Ten Commandments from God aren't the Ten *Suggestions*, this directive from Paul outlining the will of God isn't a suggestion, either—although some people treat it like it is!

Paul began by stating, "I exhort *therefore*...." When a verse says "therefore," it is referring to something that came before it. In this case, it refers to First Timothy 1:18, where Paul said to Timothy, *"This charge* [or commandment] *I commit unto thee, son Timothy."*

A charge is a commandment, and it brings responsibility with it. Paul continues, *"according to the prophecies, which went before on thee, that thou by them mightest war a good warfare."* Timothy was fighting the good fight of faith, doing the will of God, and continuing to believe and stand, holding faith and a good conscience by obeying the charge he was given.

Paul exhorted Timothy to pray all kinds of prayers: (1) supplications, (2) prayers, (3) intercessions, and (3) giving of thanks.

Supplications are definite requests. This means you can ask God to do things for people. You can ask Him to strengthen them and give them wisdom. You can pray that they will receive it and have strength for the task they are charged with accomplishing.

If you were standing in the office of the President of the United States, would you need strength? The person in that position works from dawn until way past dark every day and sometimes gets interrupted in the middle of the night, depending on what is going on in the world.

PRAYING FOR LEADERS

No person, Christian or not, has enough wisdom to be a leader in this world without the wisdom of God. So pray that the President will receive godly wisdom and strength. Pray that he will receive direction and be led by God in what he does, what kind of decisions he makes, and how he leads this nation.

Instead of complaining about the fact that the President doesn't believe exactly like you do, pray that he will lead the nation in a path of righteousness. If Christians go around complaining about the President all the time, it will short circuit their prayers for him!

Intercessions indicate prayers for people who are lost. In effect, when we pray for leaders, we are praying that the Gospel will reach the lost.

Giving of thanks should be made for *everyone*. Paul did not restrict this list to praying for kings and those in authority; he included all persons. However, we must start by praying for those who are in authority, because their actions affect all others.

This takes faith. If you don't see what you want to see happening in the government of your nation or some other nation you are praying for, it takes faith to believe that God hears and answers your prayers, and He can overcome what you are seeing. What you see doesn't always agree with what you want, does it? But God can turn things around in such situations.

In one year, because those five East German pastors started praying for their leadership instead of praying against it, they saw that nation's history change. It was headed on the wrong path, but God it turned around.

We should be making prayers and intercessions and giving of thanks for kings and all who are in authority so the Gospel will reach all men. Another reason is given in verse 2: *"That we may lead a quiet and peaceable life in all godliness and honesty."*

A QUIET AND PEACEABLE LIFE

Why should we pray to lead a quiet and peaceable life? If we are engaged in all kinds of strife, warfare, and other worldly things going on around us, they steal our time. We need to be able to devote our time to something more important—working for the kingdom of God.

We don't need to be in a constant state of turmoil caused by the world around us, up one minute and down the next, fighting all kinds of unprofitable battles.

Instead, we need to live a quiet and peaceable life in all godliness and honesty, the scripture says, *"For this is good and acceptable in the sight of God our Saviour."*

The fact that Jesus Christ is the Savior of mankind is what Paul wants emphasized right here. Is it so only kings will hear the truth of the Gospel? No, it is so *all* mankind will hear it. But if kings don't hear the Gospel, it will be harder for all to hear it. As we saw in verses 3 and 4:

1 TIMOTHY 1:3-4

3 For this is good and acceptable in the sight of God our Saviour;

4 Who will have all men to be saved, and to come unto the knowledge of the truth.

TAKING THE GOSPEL TO "ALL FLESH"

On the Day of Pentecost, Peter spoke of an Old Testament prophecy given by Joel:

ACTS 2:16–17

1 But this is that which was spoken by the prophet Joel;

2 And it shall come to pass in the last days, saith God, I will pour out of my Spirit upon all flesh.

That is what we should be asking God to do: "Send the rain, Lord. Send the former and the latter rain in the first month. Send it quickly. Send it powerfully. Send it to all nations. Send it to every nation, every tribe, every tongue, and every kindred, because I can see in the Word that this is what You want done. Most of all, send it to places where they have never heard it even once."

We haven't been diligent enough in desiring that the Gospel reach all people. We have been very diligent to take the Gospel over and over again to some people, but we have left others completely out of it.

God wants them to hear the "good news," too, and it is our responsibility to take it to them. How many believers are charged with doing this? Not just missionaries; *every* believer is charged with sharing the Gospel.

Our heart should be attuned to Psalm 2:8, which says:

PSALM 2:8

8 Ask of me, and I shall give thee the heathen for thine inheritance, and the uttermost parts of the earth for thy possession.

I'm glad we have a many-faceted inheritance. I'm glad it includes things in the natural realm as well as the spiritual realm. Consider our spiritual inheritance. What is going to last forever—the house we live in, the clothes we are wearing, and the car we are driving? Although all these things seem important to us today, they are not eternally important.

WHAT IS IMPORTANT ETERNALLY?

What is important eternally? That we are obedient in fulfilling the will of God so we will have an eternal reward. Thank God we have a temporal reward. I'm glad for it, and I'm glad that it increases. I'm glad we are blessed so we can be a temporal blessing to others, but we also ought to be a spiritual blessing to others. That's the most important thing we can do, and it starts with prayer.

1 TIMOTHY 2:3–6

3 God our Saviour...
4 Will have all men to be saved, and to come unto the knowledge of the truth.
5 For there is one God, and one mediator between God and men, the man Christ Jesus;
6 Who gave himself a ransom for all, to be testified in due time.

Daniel knew it would take 70 years for the Hebrews to get out of captivity. Today you and I know it is high time for the whole world to hear the Gospel. In fact, it's long overdue!

It's not right that 2000 years have gone by in the Age of Grace and half the world has never yet heard the Gospel. It's not the will of God. A huge job remains to be done; however, God is overcoming this situation. The Gospel is going forth into those unreached parts of the world today, and wonderful things are happening.

A PLAN FOR INDIA

Two good friends of mine are full-time missionaries in the nation of India. They are doing a work there that is second to none I have ever encountered. They are associated with one church and one Bible school in India and have opened more than 40 outreach centers in the southern part of the country.

More than six million people have been saved in their ministry in the past six years. God gave them a plan for the nation of India that they are executing, and it's obviously working.

They are reaching out into little villages previously unreached by the Gospel. And they are opening churches or outreach centers with buildings, pastors, and everything else, including enough money to operate that church for a year when the missionaries leave them. These churches, in turn, reproduce themselves. This plan is really working!

There is only one drawback. During the six years my friends ministered in India, six million Indians were saved. But during that same period of time, *forty* million more Indians were born!

We are grateful that good things are happening in unreached areas, but they need to happen on an even larger scale in order for the Gospel to reach the whole world.

Many believers are taking the responsibility to share the Gospel wherever God places them in the Body of Christ. His desire is to reach the world with this Gospel, and He will do it quickly, because He will do it most supernaturally in these end times.

"LIFTING UP HOLY HANDS"

Paul continues in verse 5:

1 TIMOTHY 2:5–8

5 For there is one God, and one mediator between God and men, the man Christ Jesus;

6 Who gave himself a ransom for all, to be testified in due time.

7 Whereunto I am ordained a preacher, and an apostle, (I speak the truth in Christ, and lie not;) a teacher of the Gentiles in faith and verity.

8 I will therefore that men pray every where, lifting up holy hands, without wrath and doubting.

Paul wants all believers, wherever they are, to lift up holy hands and pray *"without wrath and doubting."*

I don't have much trouble believing God to direct the President, because I have seen Him do it again and again, but it doesn't seem prayers for Congress always get answered the way we want them to.

PRAYERS REQUIRING MORE FAITH

I think it takes more faith to pray for those hundreds of Congressmen than it does to pray for many other things, because the political system has been so corrupted. It doesn't work the way it was organized to work. It doesn't do what it used to do.

Furthermore, the judicial system in this country is neither equitable nor just, and it is not accomplishing what God intended it to do when He gave wisdom to the founders of this nation to establish it.

To pray for our political system in faith, you need to have a great deal of knowledge of the Word of God, and you must focus on the Word more than you do on the 5 o'clock news and whatever else tells you what the government is failing to do.

We can overcome. God didn't say, "Pray for government except in the last days." We are in the last days. Perilous times have come, as Paul predicted in Second Timothy, but that does not mean our prayer is not effectual.

The effectual fervent prayer of a righteous man avails what? *Much*, and it makes tremendous power available. It makes angelic ministry available for the people for whom we are praying.

We need to pray that God will protect our leaders. There are unbalanced people loose in society who are capable of doing bizarre things. One man stuck an AK47 through the White House fence and started shooting at the White House. He didn't hit any people, but he did hit the building. And just before that, another man crashed an airplane on the front lawn of the White House!

PRAYING A PROTECTIVE HEDGE

The devil can use people like that to shoot at Presidents and other leaders. However, if you pray for God to put a hedge around the President and other leaders, the efforts of unbalanced people won't work. They will form the weapons, but those weapons won't prosper, because you prayed.

Why pray for the President's protection? We don't want him to be killed, because then we would have chaos. We would eventually have anarchy. We have never lived in conditions like that in this country, and we have no idea what it is really like.

But if we read history, we will find out what it is like, and we won't want to live in anarchy. We will want the government to be blessed, and we will want to pray the blessings of God upon those in government.

If we will do that, we will have the best conditions possible. Although everything will not be perfect, we will have what we need to do the will of God while we are here on earth, we will have the peace and quiet to do it in, and we will have help when we need it from our government.

These scriptures tell us how to pray for government: Proverbs 25:3–5, Proverbs 16:12–13, and Proverbs 21:1.

PROVERBS 25:3–5

3 The heart of kings is unsearchable.

4 Take away the dross from the silver, and there shall come forth a vessel for the finer.

5 Take away the wicked from before the king, and his throne shall be established in righteousness.

PROVERBS 16:12–13

12 It is an abomination to kings to commit wickedness: for the throne is established by righteousness.

13 Righteous lips are the delight of kings; and they love him that speaketh right.

PROVERBS 21:1

1 The king's heart is in the hand of the Lord, as the rivers of water: he turneth it whithersoever he will.

CHANGING THE KING'S HEART

When does the Lord change the king's heart? When you pray. He doesn't do it automatically; it happens when you do what God told you to do. God will change the king's will. Can God do that? Yes, He can.

He changed your will, He changed mine, and He can change the heart of a king or a leader, too.

Pray for these people to have wisdom, as Proverbs chapter 8 teaches, because you can see it takes wisdom for peaceful circumstances to prevail. (Also see Proverbs 28:2, Psalm 140:11, and Jeremiah 29:7, 11.)

I know of a number of ministers who have changed the destiny of nations simply through prayer. I have already shared with you the story of the five East German pastors who prayed for their leaders and their situation turned around. Now I am going to tell you the story of two African pastors who changed the destiny of their nation.

During the last week of July 1983, some colonels in the army and air force of Kenya decided to express their dissatisfaction with President Daniel Moi's regime by staging a coup d'etat and removing him from power.

Fifteen of them called on him and said, "We have taken control of the military forces and your police. There is no way you can resist us. Pack up and get out of the country; we're taking over. If you don't leave, we'll kill you and your associates."

TWO PRAYING BISHOPS SAVE THEIR COUNTRY

As President Moi began to pack, he thought about this ultimatum, and he remembered two friends of his who were bishops of Full Gospel denominations in his country. Bishop Washington Ngaya was one of them.

The president called the bishops and told them what had happened. He knew they were powerful in prayer. They immediately got on their knees and pled their case with God.

They said, "This man, President Moi, has been a good president. He has helped us preach the Gospel in this nation, Lord. He has even given us halls in which to hold meetings. He has given us authority to travel throughout the country.

"He has given us all kinds of help to preach the Gospel in this nation, and it isn't right for these men to take power from him unlawfully. We are unable to do anything about it, but we ask that You would help us keep this man in office."

Bishop Ngaya told this story to me and another Rhema instructor the next month at Rhema Bible Training College in Tulsa. He said, "We didn't know it at the time, but at the exact time we were praying, those 15 colonels were holding a meeting to decide which one of them would be the next president."

AMBUSHED BY ANGELS

Do you remember the time when the inhabitants of Moab, Ammon, and Mount Seir decided they would invade and take away Israel's inheritance? Ambushments were set against them in the spirit world, it says in Second Chronicles 20, and they fell upon each other and destroyed each other. Angels set those ambushments.

The same thing happened in Kenya. The 15 colonels had the power to take over, but when it came down to decide which of them was going to be the new head of state, they couldn't agree, because those two bishops were praying. God ambushed the rebels!

The discussion got so heated, the colonels took out their guns and began shooting at each other! Quite a few of them were killed—and that ended the coup.

President Moi unpacked his bags, and remained President of Kenya until 2002. Two men on their knees before God changed the destiny of a whole nation!

CONFIDENCE IN PRAYER

When the devil asks you, "What good does it do for you to pray?" tell him this story. Tell him, "I know of people who have prayed, and it changed the destiny of whole nations. And when I pray, I have the same confidence, because I am asking according to God's will, and I know He hears me. I also know I have the petition I am asking for."

The devil will try to discourage you by showing you people who aren't doing right, but that's not the point. Tell the devil, "It is written."

If you will believe what God says and act on what you know is true—no matter what you are facing, no matter who is in office, and no matter which political agenda seems to be gaining ground—you can do something about it through prayer!

PRAY, DON'T COMPLAIN

Instead of sitting around complaining about your country's political situation, moaning, "Woe is us! Judgment is about to fall," pray for your leaders, and you will find the situation will turn around.

It's more important who you PRAY for than who you VOTE for. This does not mean you shouldn't vote; it means that voting is a minor thing compared to praying for political leaders. You have power with God! You have favor with God!

Remember, Abraham prayed for Sodom and Gomorrah, and because he was in covenant relationship with God, God told him, "Abraham, I will give you anything you ask for." You have the same place with God! In fact, you have a better place and covenant with God, founded on better promises, according to Hebrews 8:6.

This means you have a responsibility to use what you know in order to pray effectually. When you do, angels of God go forth at the sound of your voice to perform what you ask.

Can angels protect a head of state from assassination plots? Of course they can. Can they give a leader wisdom when he needs it? Certainly.

In the next chapter, we will see how angels affect God's economy. That is a little closer to where you live.

9

How Angels Affect God's Economy

PSALM 103:1–5

1 Bless the Lord, O my soul: and all that is within me, bless his holy name.
2 Bless the Lord, O my soul, and forget not all his benefits:
3 Who forgiveth all thine iniquities; who healeth all thy diseases;
4 Who redeemeth thy life from destruction; who crowneth thee with loving-kindness and tender mercies;
5 Who satisfieth thy mouth with good things; so that thy youth is renewed like the eagle's.

I spend a lot of time in Psalm 103. There are many things mentioned here that relate to my daily life, so I keep it before my eyes.

The things mentioned in this Psalm are God's will for you. As you walk in Him, all of this is manifested to you. Verses 20 through 22 show more about how angels do God's pleasure for you and how they minister for you. As we know from Hebrews 1:14, angels are sent forth to minister for believers.

PSALM 103:20–22

20 Bless the Lord, ye his angels, that excel in strength that do his commandments, hearkening unto the voice of his word.
21 Bless ye the Lord, *all ye his hosts;* ye ministers of his, that *do his pleasure.*
22 Bless the Lord, all his works in all places of his dominion: bless the Lord, O my soul.

Roads to Prosperity

One of the ways you need help in this world and its kingdoms is in the realm of prosperity. God can bless you through the church. He can talk to people in the church, and they can and will bless you in the way of giving, but God can go a lot further than that if you will believe it.

Proverbs 13:22 says that the wealth of the sinner is laid up for the just! This is just one of many such scriptures we will study in this chapter. You need to know these scriptures, because you need a good foundation to stand on to receive whatever it is you are believing God for. And the bigger the thing you are believing the Lord for, the more foundation you need.

Over the years of my Christian walk, I have seen many examples of God's provision. I have not only seen supernatural provision happen in my own life; I have seen it happen in the lives of other ministries.

One example occurred in the life of Oral Roberts. In 1988, Brother Roberts was believing God for a large sum of money to keep the City of Faith operating.

Brother Roberts went on television and explained to people the importance of his obeying God. A man in Florida heard him and decided he would fly to Tulsa and give him some money. And he did.

When the man landed, the local media interviewed him, because it was a newsworthy event. Many people did not believe Brother Roberts could raise that much money.

"SOMETHING MADE ME HELP HIM"

The man from Florida said, "I've come here to help Oral Roberts. I heard he is raising some money and he needs help, and I decided I'd help him. Something made me feel like I ought to help him."

Standing there puffing on a big cigar, the man continued, "I'm not a Christian at all—I'm a dog track owner—but I felt like I ought to help him, so I came here, and I've got a check to give him." He held it up to the cameras, and it was for $1,300,000. The check was good, too. This man didn't give the money to get publicity. He said, "Something just made me feel like I ought to help him."

What was that "something" that made an unsaved man feel that way? Angelic beings! That's what they do. They contact the world for you—for your benefit. They touch things in the world system for your benefit.

As a result, people will do things for you they wouldn't ordinarily do. That's called "favor." God can give you favor with people. A car dealer once told a minister I know, "I know that God will bless my business if I bless you."

Here was another man who did not profess to be a Christian, but he knew enough about God from some source to know that God would bless him if he blessed the minister—and he believed it and acted upon it.

We read in Proverbs 13:22, *"the wealth of the sinner is laid up for the just"*—for those who *are* in rightstanding with God.

In Proverbs 16:7, we find a scripture that is part of the interpretation of this verse:

PROVERBS 16:7
7 When a man's ways please the Lord, he maketh even his enemies to be at peace with him.

This refers to those who would naturally be his enemies; those who are not kin to him; those who are not like him spiritually. Thus, God makes even those who hold opposite views to yours to be at peace with you if your ways are pleasing to Him. He gives you favor with other people.

FAVOR WITH MAN

Proverbs 3:1 tells us: *"My son, forget not my law; but let thine heart keep my commandments."*

Think of this as it applies to believers. We are not keeping the Mosaic covenant; we are keeping God's commandments. For one thing, He told us to love one another. For another, He commanded us to walk in faith and obedience toward Him.

PROVERBS 3:2-4
2 For length of days, and long life, and peace, shall they add to thee.
3 Let not mercy and truth forsake thee: bind them about thy neck [the Word of God]; write them upon the table of thine heart:
4 So shalt thou find favour and good understanding in the sight of God and man.

When your ways are God's ways, He will give you favor with man. You will find that favor by walking in God's ways and believing Him.

ANGELS ARE THE LINK

How do you receive anything from God? It's by the grace of God through faith. In this case, angels are the instrument of delivering that grace to you. They are the link between you and the kingdoms of this world for your prosperity, success, and blessing.

Why can God do that? Because He owns the whole world. This world is His. *"The earth is the Lord's and the fulness thereof,"* the Bible says. He owns the whole planet. It's His; it never was the devil's. The devil got authority to operate in it from Adam, but he never owned it.

The earth has always been God's, and it still is. The cattle on a thousand hills are His. The gold and the silver in the hills are His.

Is it difficult for Him to deliver any of that to you? No. If you are hungry, He will give you a "cow." If you are needy, He will give you some of that gold and silver—maybe in a little different form—but that's how it works.

It's His to give; it's not the devil's. It doesn't belong to anyone except God. Other people have the temporary use of it, but that's about as far as it goes.

When we go to be with the Lord, we will not take any of the gold, the silver, or even the cattle with us. They are to be used in this earthly realm. They are necessary in this world. They won't be necessary in Heaven.

GOD'S WILL FOR YOU IS PROSPERITY

God is able to prosper you in many different ways. Do you believe that? We find examples of this truth throughout the Bible. I want to show you enough scriptures so you will have no doubt in your mind what the will of God is concerning your prosperity.

Psalm 49:6 speaks of people who *"trust in their wealth, and boast themselves in the multitude of their riches."* The passage continues:

PSALM 49:7, 10

7 None of them can by any means redeem his brother, nor give to God a ransom for him.

10 For he seeth that wise men die, likewise the fool and the brutish person perish, and leave their wealth to others.

You might as well be one of the "others." You can be, if you believe this. Let's look further.

ECCLESIASTES 2:26

26 For God giveth to a man that is good in his sight wisdom, and knowledge, and joy; but to the sinner he giveth travail, to gather and to heap up, that he may give to him that is good before God.

That's what God gives to you. The kingdom of God is not meat and drink, but righteousness, joy, and peace in the Holy Spirit, and He has given the kingdom to you. He has made you able to partake of everything in the kingdom—everything it is His will for you to have.

To the sinner he gives travail (hard work) to gather riches so the sinner may give those riches to people who are good before God. I don't think we've even begun to tap in to what God wants us to have in this area, but there is plenty of testimony in the Word of God that He wants us to be prosperous.

PROVERBS 28:8

8 He that by usury and unjust gain increaseth his substance, he shall gather it for him that will pity the poor.

Do you pity the poor? How about "the poor in spirit"—those who do not know the truth? Do you pity those who have never heard the Gospel? Then God wants to bless and prosper you in the work that He has given you to do to reach them. *Those who get money unjustly gather it for those who will pity the poor.*

NO GET-RICH-QUICK SCHEME

Just in case you think God has some get-rich-quick scheme like the world has, read Third John 2, where we find that God prospers us as our soul prospers: *"Beloved, I wish above all things that thou mayest prosper and be in health, even as thy soul prospereth."*

The more your mind is renewed—the less fleshly your thinking is—the more prosperity God will put in your hands, and vice versa.

The less you renew your mind and walk in the truth of God's Word, the less you will proper. Why? Because it would be a snare, a trap, and a stumbling block to you if you are still thinking like the world thinks. You must pray about and ponder what God wants you to do with money that might come into your possession.

A GOOD SAYING

There is a saying about this that I like very much: "God will get it *TO* you if He can get it *THROUGH* you." If you simply want to gather, heap up, and hang onto money and possessions, that's no different from the way the world acts.

However, if God can see that you are prospered in your soul to the point where you realize He is blessing you and giving you abundance so you can be liberal in giving, you'll have money. But He isn't going to give things to you that will cause you to stumble.

As Jesus said in Matthew 6:33:

MATTHEW 6:33
33 But seek ye first the kingdom of God, and his righteousness; and all these things [all of the natural blessings] shall be added unto you.

You must act in that order. You must *first* seek for the purpose of God's kingdom and the purpose of His righteousness; *then* all these other things will be added to you.

But he who seeks things or makes haste to be rich—he who is in a hurry to have a big bank account and the trappings of riches—shall not be innocent.

THE WAY TO PROSPER

When the soul is prospered, the natural man will also be prospered abundantly. In other words, as Proverbs 28:20–22 says:

PROVERBS 28:20–22
20 A faithful man shall abound with blessings: but he that maketh haste to be rich shall not be innocent.
21 To have respect of persons is not good: for for a piece of bread that man will transgress.
22 He that hasteth to be rich hath an evil eye, and considereth not that poverty shall come upon him.

The same thing that happens to the wicked man will happen to the greedy man! If money comes to him, he won't be able to keep it, because he does not properly value what he has.

He values what God has given him more than he values the God Who gave it to him and what God's purpose for it is.

Don't be in a hurry to get rich! I'm not sharing a get rich-quick scheme with you. However, if you will walk in the light of God's Word for God's purpose for your life, all the things you are believing for will happen.

This is brought out clearly in Job chapter 27, where Job was discussing the plight of men who are not right with God.

JOB 27:13–15
13 This is the portion of a wicked man with God, and the heritage of oppressors, which they shall receive of the Almighty.
14 If his children be multiplied, it is for the sword: and his offspring shall not be satisfied with bread.
15 Those that remain of him shall be buried in death: and his widows shall not weep.

It is not a good testimony when you finally "kick the bucket," and your wife rejoices, saying something like, "Hallelujah! The old goat finally died!" She does not mourn for you when you die; she is relieved.

JOB 27:16–17

16 Though he [that kind of a man] heap up silver as the dust, and prepare raiment as the clay;

17 He may prepare it, but the just shall put it on, and the innocent shall divide the silver.

BELIEVE FOR PROSPERITY

Is that the will of God? Yes. The Word of God is the will of God. This wicked man may heap up treasure on earth, but it will eventually pass into your hands.

"I haven't seen much of it yet."

Have you believed it yet? Have you believed and expected it to happen? Have you dispatched angels to go and get it for you? Have you commanded them in the sense that you believed and spoke the Word of God? Don't pray to angels; commission them by believing it is possible.

PRAYING FOR FINANCIAL HELP

When my wife and I came to Rhema Bible Training College in the fall of 1978, we took Dr. Kennith Stewart's class called "Foundations of Faith." It was a rather diverse class, covering many theological truths, including the one we are studying.

Dr. Stewart mentioned how the angels of God minister for you, touching things in the natural realm for your benefit. After he finished this teaching, he had the whole class stand up and pray.

He said, "I know many of you are standing there in need of receiving financial help. We are going to pray right now that the angels of God will go forth as we do, because we are going to pray scripturally and believe we receive what God has provided.

"When we pray," he cautioned, "don't try to tell God how to do it. Let God take care of that. You believe that He will do it, and believe that the angels of God will go forth on your behalf and bring money, riches, and wealth to you to meet your needs.

"It will happen in many different ways. God might give you favor with your employer. He might give you an unexpected pay increase or a promotion to a better-paying position. Many things like that can happen because you are believing. What makes people change their mind about you or makes them give you favor? The angels are the connection. They are there to influence people, and they can do it."

THE ANSWER COMES

We did what Dr. Stewart said. We prayed and commissioned the angels to go forth and bring back what we needed. That was in October 1978. A few weeks after that, June and I went back to our apartment at lunchtime, and I went to the post office for our mail while she prepared lunch.

Among our stack of mail was a registered letter from the Pima County Treasurer in Tucson, Arizona. I had once owned some land in that county, but when I was divorced years before, I thought that land had passed from my control. I never heard anything from the county after that, so I never paid any attention to it.

The letter stated that my 10 acres had been put up for sale for seven years' worth of back taxes I owed. It went on to say that a certain man had paid the taxes, and on the next day the land would pass to him if I didn't redeem it. It stated that I owed $575.

When you're going to Bible school, you don't have $575 laying around. June and I were both working to pay for our double tuition. I could come up with the $75, but I didn't have the $500.

COMMITTING THE PROBLEM TO GOD

I brought the mail home and showed it to June. Sitting there at the table, we committed the problem to God in prayer. Then, while I was eating lunch and going through the rest of the mail, I found a letter from a man who had bought a house I owned in California.

Tenants had completely wrecked the house. It was unlivable. I had started to make repairs on it, but I had to give up when we moved to Oklahoma to attend Rhema.

God put it in a man's heart to buy this unlivable house. He came to me and said, "I want to buy your house." I said, "Have you looked at that house?" He said, "Yes. I like the location very much." It was in a nice location out in the country.

I said, "Yes, but it's not livable." He said, "That's all right. We'll take it like it is, if the price is right." I said, "I'll make you a good price." (I would have had to keep making payments on it, and I wouldn't have gotten any rent from it.)

I gave the man a good price, and he gave me a down payment, which helped us move to Oklahoma. Then this letter arrived from him.

He wrote, "I just felt like I should pay a little more on the house than what I agreed to pay you." Enclosed was his check for $500!

NOT A COINCIDENCE

This was not a coincidence! Furthermore, the letter I had received from the Pima County Treasurer had been sent to four previous addresses and was returned with "Address Unknown" marked on it each time. The clerk in that treasurer's office was more diligent than any clerk in any treasurer's office I've ever heard of. She had started trying to reach me that summer.

Someone at my last address noted on the envelope that I was retired from the U.S. Air Force and they should check with the Denver Accounting and Finance Center, which sent my retirement checks, for my current address. The clerk did so, got my current address, sent the letter again, and I received it in Oklahoma the day before the deadline.

Now I had the money. I took the check for $500, scraped up the $75, got a money order, and mailed it by registered mail to the Pima County Treasurer to redeem the property.

In the meantime, I called one of our classmates who had a sister in Tucson who was a real estate agent. I said, "Do you suppose your sister would know the current value of that property?"

He said, "Oh, yes, she will know." I called her, and she told me my property was worth between $12,000 to $15,000. I had paid about $2,800 for it many years before, and it had appreciated a great deal.

REDEEMED IN THE NICK OF TIME

You can go to a county treasurer's office, review the delinquent tax list, and pay the back taxes on any delinquent property. If it is not redeemed by a certain date, it becomes yours just because you paid the taxes.

Mr. So-and-so had paid the taxes on my property, but the notice came to me on the last possible day, telling me that if I paid the back taxes, the property would revert to me and Mr. So-and-so's money would be refunded to him.

My registered letter with the money order was post marked the day before the deadline. About two weeks later, I received a receipt, informing me my property had been redeemed and was now back in my full control. The letter also stated that they had refunded the taxes Mr. So-and-so had paid.

Mr. So-and-so wasn't happy with that. A valuable piece of property, for which he had paid only $575, had slipped through his fingers. He claimed my payment had not arrived by the deadline, hired a lawyer, and sued the county treasurer, June, and me!

But Mr. So-and-so had made a mistake: He sued the county treasurer. I received a summons to appear in court in Tucson. I got the name of a lawyer in Tucson, but he wanted at least $1,000 to take my case. I wrote to the court and explained that I was in school in Tulsa, and it was important to me not to miss any of my classes, so I wasn't going to appear.

AN ATTORNEY'S OFFER

About a week later, during the 45 minutes we were home for lunch, I received a telephone call from the Pima County Attorney. He said he would be representing the Pima County Treasurer in Mr. So-and-so's lawsuit.

He said, "I noticed on this paperwork that he is also suing you. Have you hired a lawyer?" I explained I had tried to, but I couldn't afford to, and I had written a letter to the court, explaining why I would not be able to appear.

The county attorney said, "It would be a much neater package if I represented all three of you. Would it be all right with you if I represent you in court?"

I said, "What will it cost?" He said, "Nothing. I'll do it because it makes a much neater package."

I said, "Well, praise the Lord. Feel free to represent us. Go right ahead. Represent us all you want!"

TOUCHED BY ANGELS

He went to court and represented the three of us very well, because he won. The judge decided in our favor, and Mr. So-and-so was out more money. He was so angry, he appealed. The case went from the district court to the state court of appeals. The county attorney represented us again, and he won again.

But Mr. So-and-so still wasn't satisfied. He appealed to the Arizona Supreme Court. He wanted to prove he was right. Think what this was costing him in legal fees.

The county attorney represented us the third time, and he won again. And that was the end of it. Mr. So-and-so didn't want to go to the U.S. Supreme Court.

The county attorney's willingness to represent us was more favor than man would normally give you—a lot more—and it was not just coincidence.

We had prayed in that class, and God knew that plot of land legally belonged to me, even though I didn't know it. So it came back to me. We sold it, paid many debts, and it helped make our second year at school a great deal easier.

Who touched all those people to help us? Angels did. Who influenced all those people to do what they did? Angels did. People don't normally volunteer to help you with a legal case. *Something* was contacting them and influencing them to give us favor. Angels are more than capable of doing so.

EXTRAORDINARY FAVOR FOR SLAVES

Another example of angelic help is found in Exodus, where God gave the children of Israel favor with their Egyptian slave masters. It wasn't through the goodness of their hearts, either, because the Egyptians didn't have any goodness in their hearts.

People in the world don't have anything right in their hearts. An outside, external influence must be exerted on them, and that is what angels do. They influence the outward man to do things he should do for you.

It's different with a Christian. God can talk to a believer, and because the believer has a right heart, he hears and obeys God without the need for the outside influence of angels.

SOMETHING UNUSUAL

In Exodus chapter 3, God told the children of Israel something unusual He would do for them.

EXODUS 3:19–21

19 And I am sure that the king of Egypt will not let you go, no, not by a mighty hand.

20 And I will stretch out my hand, and smite Egypt with all my wonders which I will do in the midst thereof: and after that he will let you go.

21 And I will give this people [Israel] favour in the sight of the Egyptians: and
it shall come to pass, that, when ye go, ye shall not go empty.

Why wouldn't the king of Egypt want to let the children of Israel
leave Egypt? Because they were all slaves, producing for him. They
had been pressed into slavery, and the Egyptians made their labors
more and more difficult as time went on. They were working themselves to the bone for the king, and he was getting all the benefits of
their labor.

FAITH LIKE NOAH'S

Thinking about it in the natural, it wasn't likely that the Jews would
be able to take anything of the fruits of their labors with them out of
Egypt, but it happened! God's instructions in Exodus 3 continued:

EXODUS 3:22
22 But every woman shall borrow of her neighbour, and of her that sojourneth
in her house, jewels of silver, and jewels of gold, and raiment: and ye shall
put them upon your sons, and upon your daughters; and ye shall spoil the
Egyptians.

I am sure that when God said that to Moses it seemed as unlikely in
the natural as when He told Noah it was going to rain and there was
going to be a flood on the earth. It had never rained, and Noah didn't
know what a flood was! Noah had to believe what God said, contrary
to everything in his own understanding. So did Moses, and so did the
people of Israel.

Evidently they did believe it, because look what happened in Exodus 12:35. After all the signs and wonders had come to pass, the Bible
says the Lord called for Moses and Aaron by night and said:

EXODUS 12:31, 35
31 Rise up, and get you forth from among my people.

35 And the children of Israel did according to the word of Moses; and they
borrowed of the Egyptians jewels of silver, and jewels of gold, and raiment.

SPOILING THE FOE

If the Hebrews had asked their masters for jewels and clothing, do you think those Egyptians would have given such things to them? Of course not. They would have laughed at their slaves and thrown them out of their houses. However, by this time the Hebrews were impressed by God to obey His unusual instructions, and this is what happened.

EXODUS 12:36

36 And the Lord gave the people favour in the sight of the Egyptians, so that they lent unto them such things as they required. And they spoiled the Egyptians.

Then the Bible describes what the Jews took out of Egypt: all the jewels, silver, and gold they could carry. They didn't leave the country as poverty-stricken slaves; they left as a wealthy people! *God recompensed them for all their years of servitude.*

That's *supernatural* favor. Don't try to make people favor you. Let God do it for you, because He is the Persuader. You can talk to people until you're blue in the face, and they won't listen to you. However, if you let God do it, it will come to pass just like He said it would.

The wealth of the sinner is laid up for you! And the angels of God are the link between your believing that and its coming to pass. They will see to it that it comes to pass.

Don't try to figure out how God is going to bless you. Let God take care of that. You wouldn't know how to do it, anyway. If you tried to make it happen, you would just mess it up.

The more impossible it is, the easier it is to believe for. If it looks possible, we might try to figure out how to make it happen, but when it looks absolutely *impossible*, that's the best time to believe. You just believe it, and God will bring it to pass. He is watching over His Word to perform it. You be the one who believes His Word, and you will see Him perform it.

MORE WEALTH THAN THEY COULD CARRY

One other notable example is in Second Chronicles chapter 20, which tells how three nations—Moab, Ammon, and Mount Seir—combined forces to dispossess the children of Israel from their inheritance. But when they started, God set ambushments against them.

These enemies brought all their treasure with them. Isn't that odd? What made them do that? They probably didn't trust anyone back home. God used whatever means He had to. The armies didn't bring their treasure for themselves, as they thought; they brought it for Israel.

After they reached the place where the three nations destroyed one another, the Jews spent three days picking up all the treasure off the battlefield. That's how much there was—and the Jews didn't even have to fight for it. They didn't have to lift a finger against the Moabites, the Ammonites, or the Edomites. The three enemies destroyed each other and left all their wealth behind, just laying there waiting to be taken.

The wealth of the sinner is laid up for the just! This is not some new doctrine we came up with recently because we believe in prosperity, as we have been accused of; it has been true throughout time. It's in the Word of God—I'm not making it up—it's right there in the Bible.

10

THE NAMES OF ANGELS

Angels are referred to in many different ways in the Word of God. The Word gives the names of limited *groups* of angels, such as cherubim and seraphim, as well as the names of *individual* angels, such as Michael and Gabriel.

However, some of the ways angels are referred to are not so obvious. Do you know what a "watcher" is? Sometimes that's what angels are called. They are not only watching you; they are watching over what you pray about. Did you ever think about it that way?

If you pray for kings and those in authority, who do angels watch over? Kings and those in authority. For what? For what you have been praying for, seeing to it that it comes to pass.

It's the same way with prosperity. As you stand on the Word of God concerning your finances, and as you handle them in faith according to God's direction, angels will watch over them. Would you like to have someone help you with your finances? I would. I need it.

Another aspect of the angels' work is to ensure that the devil doesn't steal from you. Some of you may have suffered financial or material losses, but it wasn't the fault of the angels. Whenever there is a failure in receiving financial protection, angels are not at fault, and neither is God. You must be the one who missed God somehow, so face up to it.

Do the best you know how to do when you are believing God for something, but if it does not come to pass, it isn't God's fault, so don't blame Him. You can always learn something new and grow in your Christian walk. You can always overcome in the present what you have not been able to overcome in the past.

There is no problem on God's side. God has provided everything you need, and He has done all things well. He has made you able to partake of your inheritance. The only problem that could exist is on your side. That's why it is not wise to tell just anyone you have suffered a failure to receive God's provision.

They may reply, "If you'd had enough faith, you would have gotten it." There's not much compassion in that attitude.

When you come down to the bottom line, what went wrong? What broke down? You won't find the answer on God's side. He never misses it. I know He is absolutely dependable, and I am learning how to be dependable. I am His child growing to maturity in Him.

WORDS FROM ANTIQUITY

There are two words in Greek and two in Hebrew that are translated "angel" over and over again.

In Greek, the first word is *angelos*. It literally means "messenger." This word can also refer to a human being, because humans are sometimes messengers. So if a person is acting as a messenger, the Bible may refer to him by this term.

Therefore, when you see the word *angelos* in Greek, it doesn't necessarily mean "angel." You must determine its correct meaning by the context in which the word occurs.

The second Greek word for "angel" is *leitourgos*. This word is usually translated "minister." Whenever you see this word, you can also determine whether it means "angel" or human "minister" by its context.

The Hebrew word that is the counterpart of *angelos* is *malak*. That is how God refers to messengers or angels in the Old Testament. One other Hebrew word for "angel" is *misharathim,* a plural word (as indicated by the *im* ending) meaning "angels" or several "ministers."

Both words are used in Psalm 104:4: *"Who maketh his angels* [His *malak*] *spirits; his ministers* [His *misharathim*] *a flaming fire."*

UNDERSTANDING SCRIPTURE

I can't stress enough the importance of context in determining the true meaning of scripture. Next to having the Spirit of Truth Himself living in you, context is the next most important way to understand scripture.

For many years, no one had word study concordances such as Cruden's, Young's, or Strong's definitions to refer to. Although these reference books can help you a great deal, the context in which a word is found in scripture is still the most important thing.

Don't ever take the definition of a word and try to make a doctrine out of it, because men define words.

God did not write dictionaries or concordances. Beware of using Hebrew or Greek definitions of words alone to establish doctrine.

LEAN ON THE HOLY SPIRIT

Men's definitions are a help to you, but to fully understand what a scripture means, always lean on the Holy Spirit—always, always, always. Don't lean on your own understanding; just lean on the Spirit of God, and in all your ways acknowledge God. He will direct you to the truth.

The Spirit of Truth will guide you into how much truth? According to John 16:13, *"Howbeit when he, the Spirit of truth, is come, he will guide you into all truth."* And the Holy Spirit uses context more than anything else to teach you.

Again, these Greek and Hebrew words often refer to the ministry of men as well as the ministry of angels. The context will tell you the difference.

As we saw, Psalm 104:4 refers to angelic beings: *"Who maketh his angels spirits; his ministers a flaming fire."* This verse is quoted again in the New Testament, in Hebrews 1:7. Both *angelos* and *leitourgos* are found when Psalm 104:4 is quoted.

The next word is *sava*. This pictures the heavenly host employed as a military force, like an army. We call it "the heavenly host" or "the host of Heaven." Psalm 103:21 says, *"Bless ye the Lord, all ye his hosts."* That word is *sava*.

The compound names of Jehovah are instructive to us. Jehovah Rapha means "the Lord that heals you." Jehovah Tsidkenu means "the Lord your righteousness." Jehovah Shammah means "the Lord present" or "the Lord with you."

Another compound name of Jehovah is Jehovah Sabaoth. *Sabaoth* is a form of the Hebrew word *sava* or "hosts." Jesus is "the Lord of hosts."

THE CAPTAIN OF THE HOST APPEARS

JOSHUA 5:13–14

13 And it came to pass, when Joshua was by Jericho, that he lifted up his eyes and looked, and, behold, there stood a man over against him with his sword drawn in his hand: and Joshua went unto him, and said unto him, Art thou for us, or for our adversaries?

14 And he said, Nay; but as captain of the host of the Lord am I now come.

Joshua saw Jesus in the form of the Lord of hosts in a vision when Joshua was about to surround the city of Jericho by God's commandment.

The Lord of hosts was standing there accompanied by His heavenly army. Joshua walked up to Him and asked, "Are You for us or against us?" He replied, "Neither. But as captain of the Lord's hosts am I now come." In other words, He doesn't come to earth to do the biding of man; He comes to do the commandments of God as man agrees with them.

He helped the children of Israel in this case. What made the walls of Jericho fall down flat? It wasn't only because the Jews walked around the walls seven times. You can walk around walls for a long time, and they will not fall down flat.

THE GREATEST MIRACLE: SILENCE

Probably the greatest miracle in their walking around the walls for seven days is that they were *quiet* for seven days! Think about it: If you couldn't talk for 24 hours, you'd miss it. It's very hard not to talk for a long period of time.

It was miraculous that a whole army of natural men marched around the city on seven days and never said a word while they were doing it, but that's what God told them to do.

A little thing like that in the way of obedience brings a great response from God in the way of power. The walls fell down. The angelic host was there. The captain of the Lord's hosts, Jehovah Sabaoth, was there to direct the activity of the angelic host around Jericho while Israel was obeying God. He kept God's commandments, hearkening to the voice of God's Word.

In this case, God's Word did not have an audible voice. It was a voice of obedience as the army marched around the city in silence. Your lifestyle gives that testimony of obedience to angelic beings in the same way what you say does.

Another word that shows us angels is found in Psalm 68:17, *"The chariots of God are twenty thousand, even thousands of angels."* That is an innumerable number. It doesn't say exactly how many angels there are. The verse concludes, *"The Lord is among them, as in Sinai, in the holy place."*

Now look at the first verse of Psalm 68:

PSALM 68:1

1 Let God arise, let his enemies be scattered: let them also that hate him flee before him.

In this Psalm you see part of how that happens. God is lifted up and He arises in the earth to put to flight His and your enemies through the angelic ministry. *The chariots of God are angels.*

SYMBOLS OF ANGELS

In Second Kings chapter 6, we read about Elisha being surrounded by an army in the little town of Dothan, but the prophet also saw the angelic host that was present. He prayed that his servant's eyes would be opened as well.

It happened, and he saw *"the mountain was full of horses and chariots of fire round about Elisha"* (v. 17). So both horses and chariots can symbolize angelic beings.

Another example we saw that symbolizes angels somewhat is found in Daniel 4. There, Nebuchadnezzar the king had a dream that troubled him. He couldn't understand it, so he asked all his wise men—the Chaldeans, the magicians, the soothsayers, and the astrologers—for its interpretation, but they couldn't interpret it.

Then Daniel came and told the king what he had seen, and he explained the meaning to him. Daniel said in verse 17: *"This matter is by the decree of the watchers, and the demand by the word of the holy ones: to the intent that the living may know that the most High ruleth in the kingdom of men, and giveth it to whomsoever he will, and setteth up over it the basest of men."*

GOD'S ULTIMATUM TO THE KING

Daniel noted that the watchers were watching over Nebuchadnezzar and his kingdom. After this dream, God gave the king an ultimatum: He told him to humble himself before Him and stop thinking he was responsible for all his own glory, power, and might.

Nebuchadnezzar did not hearken to God's ultimatum. He walked around for a whole year with the opportunity to humble himself and repent of his attitude, but he didn't do it.

At the end of that year, the king became like a wild man. He lost his sanity. He went out and lived among the animals, crawling on all fours and eating grass, the Bible says, like oxen. His hair and his nails grew long. You can picture what he must have looked like! But at the end of seven years' time, Nebuchadnezzar regained his senses and his kingdom.

Angels have something to do with things like that. Nebuchadnezzar's madness was for his own good, and it did have a good effect in his life. Finally he did humble himself. I would rather humble myself than have God direct it. I don't want to crawl around on my hands and knees and eat grass. The Word of God tells you to humble yourself, and you can do it. Note that the watchers were involved in Nebuchadnezzar's case.

A CHANGED MAN

Daniel prayed for King Nebuchadnezzar for a long time. If you trace what happened to the king through the chapters of Daniel, you will see that he turned out to be a far different person than when he started. He was really a changed man at the end of his experience. This is the king's dramatic testimony as recorded in Daniel:

DANIEL 4:34–37

34 At the end of the days I Nebuchadnezzar lifted up mine eyes unto heaven, and mine understanding returned unto me, and I blessed the most High, and I praised and honoured him that liveth for ever, whose dominion is an everlasting dominion, and his kingdom is from generation to generation:

35 And all the inhabitants of the earth are reputed as nothing: and he doeth according to his will in the army of heaven [the angelic or heavenly host] and among the inhabitants of the earth: and none can stay his hand, or say unto him, What doest thou?

36 At the same time my reason returned unto me; and for the glory of my kingdom, my honour and brightness returned unto me; and my counsellors and my lords sought unto me; and *I was established in my kingdom, and excellent majesty was added unto me.*

37 Now I Nebuchadnezzar praise and extol and honour the King of heaven, all whose works are truth, and his ways judgment and those that walk in pride he is able to abase.

The king began to give credit where credit was due. He no longer looked at himself and thought he was something great. He no longer thought he was the biggest guy on the block.

He regained favor with God and man. He didn't have much when he was crawling around out there in the weeds. But when his reason returned to him, men recognized something in him, and they gave him favor again. The angelic host had something to do with everything that followed.

No one knew better than Nebuchadnezzar that God is able to abase those who walk in pride! He was a far different man from the man who was described in Daniel 3:19:

DANIEL 3:19
19 Then was Nebuchadnezzar full of fury, and the form of his visage was changed against Shadrach, Meshach, and Abednego.

Then, the king was enraged and full of fury, easily displeased, it seems. However, he was a different man at the end of his time of madness, and angels had something to do with it in response to Daniel's prayers for him. The Bible doesn't say the angels had everything to do with this change in a natural man like the king. Their efforts were probably similar to the way the Spirit of the Lord deals with you.

WHO IS LIKE GOD?

You will find another name for angels in Psalm 89:6: *"For who in the heaven can be compared unto the Lord? who among the sons of the mighty can be likened unto the Lord?"*

The angel Michael's very name means "Who Is Like God?" The name doesn't mean that Michael is like God in ability or majesty. God is God alone. Although you are His child, His offspring, and begotten of Him, like Him in character, and blessed by Him beyond what you can even imagine, He will always be God alone. God is God alone.

Michael's very name, "Who Is Like God," includes that question. Compare that to Satan, who went around saying, "I will be like the most High. I will exalt my kingdom above the other stars of God. I will, I will."

Michael has a totally different attitude: "Who Is Like God?" He magnifies God all the time by the very sound of his name!

That's what Psalm 89:6 is saying:

PSALM 89:6
6 For who in the heaven can be compared unto the Lord? who among the sons of the mighty can be likened unto the Lord?

That is the Hebrew phrase I want to share with you now—*bene elim,* "sons of the mighty." Those great, powerful beings that are angels—in all their glory, magnificence, and spiritual grace—are still beings *created* by God.

They are not to be compared to God in any way at all, other than in their character and the way they behave and live. They are nothing like God is in His entirety.

REVERENCING AND WORSHIPPING GOD

Verse 7 continues:

PSALM 89:7

7 God is greatly to be feared in the assembly of the saints, and to be had in reverence of all them that are about him.

Angels will always reverence and worship God, and they will always show that reverence clearly and plainly. *Bene elim* means "powerful in spirit." Angels are sons of the mighty. They are powerful in spirit, and they excel men in strength, as it says in Psalm 103.

They far surpass you in spiritual strength at this point in your existence. Someday, however, you will excel them. Are you looking forward to that? Then you will be in a position to rule over angels, the Word of God says.

There's another term similar to that used in Hebrews. It is *bene Elohim,* which means "sons of God." This is another term that can refer to either men or angels, depending on the context.

As you know, *Elohim* is a name for God: "In the beginning *Elohim* created the heaven and the earth" it says in Genesis 1:1. In the beginning, Father, Son, and Holy Ghost created the Heaven and the earth. The Godhead created all the rest of the stars and everything else in the universe. Jesus was involved in the whole creation, and *"without him was not any thing made that was made"* (John 1:3).

"SONS OF GOD": ANGELS OR MEN?

So *bene Elohim* means "sons of God." You will be able to tell from the context whether it refers to men or angels. There are places, such as Genesis 6, where the phrase definitely refers to *men.* For example, it says in verse 2: *"The sons of God saw the daughters of men that they were fair; and they took them wives of all which they chose."*

These men disobeyed God in breaking the bounds of their covenant, and they started to intermarry with unbelievers. The godly line began to disappear from the earth because of it—and it almost did before the flood came to stop it.

In Job chapter 1, you will see that the sons of God—*angelic beings* in this case—came before God on a certain day and presented themselves before Him. Satan came with them.

Because Satan is a spirit being and lives in the realm of darkness, he doesn't normally hang out with people. He came with other spirit beings, and all of them presented themselves before God in the earth. Satan could come with them before God as He appeared in the earth because he still had dominion in the earth given to him by Adam. (See also Zechariah 3:1–7.)

The term "the sons of God" is used in Job 38:4, 7: *"Where wast thou...when the morning stars sang together, and all the sons of God shouted for joy?"*

That's *bene Elohim* here, meaning "all the sons of God."

TRAVELING THE HEAVENS

Another term for angels, and one that is used quite often, especially in prophetic scripture, is "stars." Stars denote the heavenly nature and abode of angelic beings.

There are frequent references to stars in the Book of Revelation. Some symbolize angels, and some of these references refer to literal stars. Stars are bright lights. Our sun is a star, but a very small star. Our solar system was established to orbit around the sun. *Life exists only on planet Earth.* There is no life on any of the other planets.

The only time life has ever been off this planet that I am aware of is when U.S. astronauts visited our little moon, which is not too far away, compared with how far everything else is, and also when people die and go to Heaven, where God and His life abound.

The kind of speed (or escape velocity) it takes to get to the moon is about 30,000 miles an hour. You must first get accelerated to get to the moon, but you don't travel all the way there at that speed. After accelerating to escape velocity, then you decelerate from it, because of the Earth's gravitational pull.

And when you get close to the moon, you start to slowly accelerate again, because its gravitational force will pull you toward the moon. When you actually get to the moon, you will be going about 3,000 miles an hour.

"ANGEL SPEED"

Although man is able to go fast to reach the moon, he doesn't go nearly as fast as angels do. Angels travel really fast. How fast is "angel speed"? I don't know how to define it any other way, but they travel as fast as you need them; probably at the speed of thought!

If it took an angel two years to get from Heaven to Earth, it wouldn't help you much. Aside from the moon, the closest star to Earth is Alpha Centauri, two light years away. To reach that star, you would have to go at the speed of light—186,000 miles a second or approximately 366 million miles an hour—for two years!

If angels were hanging around Alpha Centauri when you needed them, that wouldn't be close enough. You wouldn't want to wait two years for an angel to come help you. When you need help, you need it immediately.

How many angels are with you all the time? I don't know. In fact, I don't know if angels are with you every second anyway—but they are always with you when you *need* them, and there is no problem with how long it takes them to get to you.

Sometimes people get confused about what the angel Gabriel told Daniel when he was delayed for 21 days fighting fallen spirits while responding to Daniel's prayers.

JESUS' TRIUMPH

Who had dominion in the earth in Daniel's time? Satan and his fallen spirits had dominion in the earth at that time, because Adam gave it to him. But who took it back? Jesus did! And who has it today? Believers do! Today it won't take *you* 21 days to get an answer to your prayers.

Many Christians have the idea that you must fight in the heavenlies to get things accomplished. But that fight has already been won!

As the Bible says in Colossians 2:15, Jesus defeated all the satanic forces openly, made a show of them openly, and triumphed over them openly.

Jesus did all this openly so you would know it, you would have the revelation of it, and you would act in faith based on what He has already done. However, He does not repeat over and over again what He has already done.

For example, if you go to the local grocery store and buy a pound of ground meat, you wouldn't take that ground meat home and grind it 15 more times, would you? It's *already* ground. But that is what some Christians try to do: They try to fight battles that Jesus has already won.

Jesus has already won the victory!

All evil spirits have been defeated!

You are in the army of occupation.

Speak the Word, and evil spirits will bow their knee to you. It doesn't take any longer than that.

They cannot withhold what you know is true from you.

If there is any delay, it comes from your mind. The delay is not because of God. Furthermore, the devil cannot stop or defeat you if you walk in the Spirit.

You are learning and growing in your understanding as you go along. Answers may not happen instantly for you yet, but that's all right; they will happen as you fight the good fight of faith.

STARS AND ANGELS

We found that stars sometimes symbolize angelic beings. As we read, Job 38 expresses that very well. In this chapter, God asked Job, "Job, where were you when all *the morning stars* sang together, all the sons of God shouted for joy, and the whole universe was in harmony?" In other words, nothing was out of harmony in all of God's creation.

In Psalm 148, you will see "stars" and "angels" referred to in the same context, but the terms are used symbolically. (When there is plain understanding also in context, don't reject the plain understanding because you also see symbolic meaning.)

PSALM 148:1–5
1 Praise ye the Lord. Praise ye the Lord from the heavens: praise him in the heights.
2 Praise ye him, all his *angels:* praise ye him, *all his hosts.*
3 Praise ye him, sun and moon: praise him, *all ye stars of light.*
4 Praise him, ye heavens of heavens, and ye waters that be above the heavens.
5 Let them [including the angelic beings and those referred to here] praise the name of the Lord: for he commanded, and they were created.

All the angels were God's creation. Remember, angels do not reproduce themselves. God also created the stars you see. They are there for a blessing, and you will understand more about this in the hereafter.

ANGELS AS "BEASTS"

Another term that is used for "angels" is found in the *King James Version* of the Book of Revelation. In chapter 4, angels are called "beasts" in Elizabethan English. That word "beast" has been translated from the Greek word *zoon,* which comes from the word *zoe* or "life"—the God-kind of life.

Most modern translations of *zoon* say something like "living creatures," not beasts. The term can be confused in Revelation, because later in the book there is another Greek word that is also translated "beasts," but it is a different word, *therion,* which means "evil, poisonous, venomous, dangerous beings."

Zoon was translated "beasts" in the *King James Version* but "living creatures" in modern translations.

The living creatures of Revelation 4 are four special angelic beings who live in the presence of God and whose special ministry there is to uplift God, to worship Him, and to point all creation to Him in worship and praise.

They continually praise and worship God, saying, *"Holy, holy, holy, Lord God Almighty, which was, and is, and is to come"* (Rev. 4:8). These living creatures represent the work of redemption, and are constantly praising God for that work and for how it is being fulfilled in the earth today.

CHERUBIM AND SERAPHIM

Those four living creatures are a special category of angel. They are much like cherubim and seraphim. *Cherubim* are seen in different places in the Bible.

In the Old Testament, for example, Moses was commanded to make replicas of cherubim and put them on the Ark of the Covenant on either side of the mercy seat, with their wings spread out, showing that they were there to bring the mercy of God to all who believed and kept the covenant. But the cherubim are real beings, not just golden replicas.

Numerous references to cherubim are also found in Ezekiel chapter 10. There you can read what God says they look like, and this description of the cherubim in Ezekiel is much like the description of the living creatures in the Book of Revelation.

The *seraphim* are angelic beings who are described in Isaiah 6:2 much like the living creatures and the cherubim. All of the seraphim have many wings, eyes, and faces. That's the best way to summarize a description of these angelic beings.

Although they may sound weird to you, if you saw one, you would not think it was weird; it would be extremely glorious.

The Bible offers a natural description of something that is supernatural, and the description may not be clear to you until you meditate on what God is really saying.

A SPECIAL MINISTRY

All of these beings—the living creatures, the cherubim, and the seraphim—have a special ministry. They proclaim, protect, take messages, show the need for man to be righteous before he can stand in the presence of God, and serve Him. They show forth God's holiness all the time. They reveal God's holiness continually in the presence of God and to man.

Two angels are named in the Word of God: *Michael* and *Gabriel.* Of course, Satan, the fallen angel, had the name *Lucifer,* which means Light Bearer, when he was created, but he no longer has it, because it is no longer appropriate for him.

As we learned earlier, Michael's name means "Who Is Like God?" and it is contrasted with Satan, who said, "I will be like the most High. I will exalt myself." That was pride, the total opposite of the way God is.

HANDLING THE DEVIL

In Jude verse 9 it says that Michael disputed with the devil about the body of Moses. He didn't malign the devil; he simply said, *"The Lord rebuke thee."*

We should handle encounters with the devil the same way. Calling him names and so forth doesn't impress him. Speak from your heart, but, like Michael, do not bring railing accusations against him.

Simply rebuke him with the Word of God: "It is written. In the name of Jesus, depart from me! Satan, you have no right to touch me or bother me!"

Gabriel means "Mighty One of God." He is a messenger. In the Book of Daniel, he appeared to Daniel. In the Gospel of Luke, he appeared to Zacharias, telling him that he and his wife would have a son, who became John the Baptist.

Gabriel also appeared to Mary, telling her of the forthcoming birth of Jesus. She believed what he said. He came from God to speak important truths to mankind at those times.

SPECIAL ASSISTANCE

Does God still do that? He still *can,* yes. Does He *need* to send you an angel all the time to give you direction? No. You should never seek to see an angel. Don't ask God to send an angel to talk to you or anything like that.

There is nothing in scripture that ever instructs you to do that. However, God may send an angel to you if you have a special need.

I would say that Mary had an unusual need. Whoever had a virgin birth before that? Whoever got pregnant before without knowing a man? Who was going to have to stand up to her fiance and her whole community, who thought she had sinned? Who was going to have to stand in faith toward God until that child was delivered and then rear Him in the right way?

Mary needed special assistance, and God gave it to her. He even sent an angel to assure Joseph that it was all right to take Mary as his wife.

If you need special assistance, you will get it, too.

OTHER ANGELS?

Before we leave this subject of *named* angels, we must clear up another point. Many other angels' names are floating around these days.

They come from contemporary books people have written. They got these names from sources *other* than the Bible. Most of the time, they got them from what we call the apocryphal books. The apocryphal books are full of names of other angels, such as Raphael, Uriel, and Jeremiel.

The Apocrypha, however, is *not* scripture. Some people calling themselves Christians maintain it is scripture, but we do not agree.

Although it was written in Elizabethan English, and its text is divided into chapter and verse like books of the Bible, the Apocrypha is not genuine scripture.

Its books were excluded from the canon after careful, prayerful deliberation by godly men at the time your Bible came into being. They were excluded because there are things in them that are not in agreement with the Word of God.

The fact that other angels are named in them is one reason why the books are not included in the Bible. That information does not agree with the rest of the Word of God! It is not revelation that came from God.

You have a name, and I am sure all the angels have names, too. However, if you get too far over into what the angels' names are, people will soon start calling on specific angels to do what that angel is supposed to do.

You should never even consider doing that! Probably to keep us from error like this, God did not name any more angels in the Bible.

You don't need to know what is in the books of the apocrypha; however, if you want to read them, it's probably all right. Put them in the same category as reading history, but don't even begin to think they are scripture. They are not.

PROPAGATING ERROR

I knew a pastor, a good man, who got into this error and thought he'd had revelations from God. He wrote a book about angels which, in effect, *added* to the Word. This is a dangerous thing to do!

That man died shortly after his book came out. His death was probably premature, because he was still middle aged. What he was doing was getting people to become dependent on angels rather than on Jesus and the Word of God. God will not allow false doctrine like that to start in the middle of a great revival!

I saw another book like his. This author described angels by their appearance. The whole book was full of sketches he drew of all the angels and demons he supposedly saw. He even gave their names and what they did.

You don't need to get into that! It's not important. Do you know what it does? It satisfies the curiosity of people's flesh. That's why bookstores sell a lot of books like this—but you don't need to buy any.

God has given you in the Word of God everything you need to know about the angels of God, demons, or anything else you will ever encounter.

STAY IN THE WORD

You don't need someone else's *experience* adding to divine revelation. I don't care if their experience was good, bad, or indifferent—it cannot add to the Word of God. Of course, if it illustrates the Word of God, that is all right.

Good Bible teachers use such illustrations all the time, but you will never find them using illustrations that go *beyond* the Word of God or *add* something to the Word of God. That is what I am warning you about.

People have frequently done that, saying, "Well, I had an *experience,* and I don't care *what* the Bible says!" This wrong attitude will get them in trouble.

You need to be fully satisfied with what God has given you in His Word. Is the Bible enough for you? It's enough for me. It's *more* than enough for me. You don't need to add to it.

For example, you don't need to read unscriptural information that angels supposedly fight each other, taking their swords and cutting off each other's wings, and so forth. Aside from being untrue, such information has nothing to do with what you are called to do.

I read one book that said angels have to fight demons if saints pray. It went on to say that sometimes the angels get wounded, so the saints have to pray for these wounded angels to be healed. Come on! Show me that in scripture. Show me where it ever said in the Word to pray for a wounded angel so he would get healed!

And do angels fight with *metal* swords? I doubt it very much. This is all man's finite thinking, trying to understand something that is *beyond* his understanding. It is not edifying, and it won't help you. In fact, it will hinder you.

Other authors say you must call angels by name so they will come and do what they are supposed to do. No, you don't. You call on the Name of Jesus. The angels then go forth and do His commandments.

Calling angels by name has nothing to do with answers to prayers. If you get off into these things, you will get off track and fall into a ditch!

11

THE ANGEL OF THE LORD

There is one description of an angelic being in the Bible that is very special and unique. We refer to this being as He appears in the earth as "the angel of the Lord."

The phrase "the angel of the Lord" is from the Hebrew *malak Yahweh*. *Yahweh* is the old Hebrew word the Jews wouldn't even pronounce; it was so holy to them. From it came the word *Jehovah*. This word definitely refers to God Himself, so the name of this being is translated "the angel (*malak*) of the Lord (*Yahweh*)."

He is the Lord Himself—the Lord Jesus Christ appearing in the earth prior to His incarnation!

Thus, when you see the term "the angel of the Lord" in the Old Testament, it may refer to Jesus Himself appearing in the earth before His incarnation. You can determine by what He does that it is He, not just by the name He is referred to.

Some try to determine the difference by whether it says "*an* angel of the Lord" or "*the* angel of the Lord," but you can't determine it that way; it's not good doctrine. Using articles such as "a" or "the" is not a safe way to interpret the Bible, because articles are often simply matters of translation.

The context will show you whether it is Jesus appearing in the earth by what He does or says about Himself. He will do or say things that only God can do or say.

For example, in one place the angel of the Lord says, "I will forgive your iniquities." Is there anyone else who can forgive your iniquities and cleanse you from your sins? Is there anyone else who would receive an offering or a sacrifice presented to Him? No, not in the kingdom of Heaven.

There are other beings, fallen beings, that would lead people astray into the darkness of the devil's kingdom, but no godly angel would.

In Exodus 3, "the angel of the Lord" accepts worship. He ascribes deity to Himself. He says He is God, and He acts as God!

There are absolute parallels in the ministry of "the angel of the Lord" with the ministry of Jesus as He walked the earth, as revealed in the four Gospels.

HE IS THE SAME!

We will see an absolute parallel between what He did when He appeared as "the angel of the Lord" in the Old Testament, what He did in the Gospels as He walked this earth, and what He does today as our High Priest. It's the same! Jesus Christ is the *same* yesterday, today, and forever, according to Hebrews 13:8.

No matter in which form He appears in the earth—whether as "the angel of the Lord" in the Old Testament or as the *man* Christ Jesus in our dispensation—He is still God!

If He appears today, how does He appear? *As He is*—the man Christ Jesus. He became a human being in the Incarnation, He has remained that way since, and He will always be the man Christ Jesus, the glorified man. He will not revert to appearing as "the angel of the Lord" as He did before the incarnation.

The parallels in Jesus' ministry before and after the incarnation occur in the areas of revelation, commission, deliverance, protection, intercession, advocacy, confirming the covenant, comfort, and judgment. We will examine each of these areas.

PARALLELS IN MINISTRY

We begin to see the parallels in two examples in Exodus, where "the angel of the Lord" appeared to Moses. In the second chapter, God heard the groaning of Israel, and He remembered His covenant with Abraham, Isaac, and Jacob.

EXODUS 2:23–25

23 And it came to pass in process of time, that the king of Egypt died: and the children of Israel sighed by reason of the bondage, and they cried, and their cry came up unto God by reason of the bondage.

24 And God heard their groaning, and God remembered his covenant with Abraham, with Isaac, and with Jacob.

25 And God looked upon the children of Israel, and God had respect unto them.

The story continues in Exodus 3:

EXODUS 3:1–4

1 Now Moses kept the flock of Jethro his father in law, the priest of Midian: and he led the flock to the backside of the desert, and came to the mountain of God, even to Horeb.

2 And *the angel of the Lord* appeared unto him in a flame of fire out of the midst of a bush: and he looked, and, behold, the bush was not consumed.

3 And Moses said, I will now turn aside, and see this great sight, why the bush is not burnt.

4 And when the Lord saw that he turned aside to see, *God called unto him* out of the midst of the bush, and said, Moses, Moses. And he said, Here am I.

GOD CALLED TO MOSES

This says it was God speaking to him, doesn't it? It says it as plainly as possible: *"God called unto him out of the midst of the bush."*

EXODUS 3:5–6

5 And he said, Draw not nigh hither: put off thy shoes from off thy feet, for the place whereon thou standest is holy ground.

6 Moreover he said, I am the God of thy father, the God of Abraham, the God of Isaac, and the God of Jacob. And Moses hid his face; for he was afraid to look upon God.

God communicated with Moses about why He had visited him and what Moses was to do in Egypt. He said in the next verse:

EXODUS 3:7–10

7 I have surely seen the affliction of my people which are in Egypt, and have heard their cry by reason of their taskmasters; for I know their sorrows;

8 And I am come down to deliver them out of the hand of the Egyptians, and to bring them up out of that land unto a good land and a large, unto a land flowing with milk and honey; unto the place of the Canaanites, and the Hittites, and the Amorites, and the Perizzites, and the Hivites, and the Jebusites.

9 Now therefore, behold, the cry of the children of Israel is come unto me: and I have also seen the oppression where with the Egyptians oppress them.

10 Come now therefore, and I will send thee.

MOSES IS SENT

God said He had come down to deliver them, but actually He sent Moses to do that. Why did He do it that way? Why didn't He do it Himself? Because man has dominion in the earth. This truth is repeated over and over again in the Bible.

God gave man that dominion by His Word, and God cannot violate His own Word. He can't come and make something happen in the earth because He's God. He will do it through the man He gave dominion to—always, always, always!

The sovereign Lord will do what He will. He will do what He said. What He will do is what He said He would do, and He won't do it differently from what He said, because that's His Word, and His Word cannot fail or be changed.

WHAT RELIGION SAYS

Religious thought says, "God can do anything He wants to." That's not true! He will accomplish everything He has said. He will accomplish everything His will has revealed, but He will do it the way He said He will. This is constantly revealed to us throughout scripture.

God said He would come down and deliver the children of Israel, but first He revealed Himself to Moses. Then, as Moses thought more about this task he was being sent to accomplish, he asked:

EXODUS 3:11
11 Who am I, that I should go unto Pharaoh, and that I should bring forth the children of Israel out of Egypt?

God began to reveal Himself even further to Moses than He had before. In this appearance, He revealed Himself in a new way:

EXODUS 3:13–14
13 And Moses said unto God, Behold, when I come unto the children of Israel, and shall say unto them, The God of your fathers hath sent me unto you; and they shall say to me, What is his name? what shall I say unto them?
14 And God said unto Moses, I AM THAT I AM: and he said, Thus shalt thou say unto the children of Israel, I AM hath sent me unto you.

REVELATION

The eternal, self-existent God, Who has always been and Who shall always be, revealed Himself in a greater degree to Moses at this point. This is the first parallel in ministry: *revelation.*

Whenever "the angel of the Lord" appeared on the earth, he brought *revelation* to mankind. When Jesus appeared to you at the moment of your new birth, what did He do for you? He brought you revelation. You received it, acted on it, and became a new creation. Revelation began within you. Your understanding was opened at that moment. God began to reveal Himself to you, and He has been doing so ever since.

Did He do that for His disciples? Did He ever show them who He was? One day He asked Peter:

MATTHEW 16:13
13 Whom do men say that I the Son of man am?

Some of the disciples replied with various names, but Peter answered in verse 16:

MATTHEW 16:16
16 Thou art the Christ, the Son of the living God.

And Jesus replied:

MATTHEW 16:17
17 Blessed art thou, Simon Bar-jona: for flesh and blood hath not revealed it unto thee, but my Father which is in heaven.

So Jesus, while walking the earth, revealed Who He was, who had sent Him, and what He had come to do. Today He is constantly revealing Himself to us by the Word of God.

In John17:6, Jesus prayed to His Father for His disciples:

JOHN 17:6
6 *I have manifested thy name* unto the men which thou gavest me out of the world: thine they were, and thou gavest them me; and they have kept thy word.

In other words, Jesus has made the Father's name manifest or known. People who keep the Word are those who have the revelation of who Jesus is.

"He that doeth truth cometh to the light," John 3:21 says. By being a doer of the Word, you are enlightened and given more revelation. Revelation is continually coming to you today like it did to Moses and Jesus' disciples in their time.

COMMISSION

What else did "the angel of the Lord" do when He came to Moses? He *commissioned* Moses to go back to Egypt to deliver the children of Israel, who were in bondage.

As Jesus walked this earth, He commissioned His own disciples. First, He commissioned 12 and sent them two by two before Him into the villages that were on His itinerary. He told them to preach the good news to the Jews (but not to the Gentiles) that the Messiah was coming, that they were free, and that they could be healed and delivered.

"Heal the sick, cleanse the lepers, raise the dead, cast out devils," He told them in Matthew 10:8—and they went out and did it!

Then He commissioned 70 more, and they went out in pairs and did the same thing. They came back rejoicing, saying, *"Lord, even the devils are subject unto us through thy name"* (Luke 10:17).

Does Jesus commission believers today? Don't we call Mark chapter 16 and Matthew chapter 28 the Great Commission? It's also found in Luke chapter 24.

We are commissioned by the Word of God today. Jesus' disciples were commissioned by Him as they walked the earth, and Moses was commissioned as "the angel of the Lord" appeared to him.

DELIVERANCE

Deliverance is the third parallel point in ministry. "The angel of the Lord" sent Moses to deliver the Jews from their Egyptian bondage.

Later He appeared to another man in the Old Testament and sent him on a mission to deliver the Jewish nation from oppression.

In Judges 6:12, "the angel of the Lord" appeared to a man named Gideon. The children of Israel had done evil in the sight of the Lord. They had not kept their covenant with God. They had not obeyed God's commandments. They may have been keeping them outwardly, but they weren't keeping them in their hearts.

In Judges 6, we find that the Midianites had raided Israel for seven years. They had oppressed the Jews and stolen whatever they could find. The Midianites were people of the desert, wandering nomads, and whenever they found a weak nation like Israel, they went there and plundered it.

The Jews had become "greatly impoverished" because of these annual raids, and they cried out to God just like they had when they were in Egypt.

God heard them and sent a prophet to them. God said, "Don't be afraid of these people. Don't worry; I will set you free." Then He began to keep His promise. In Judges 6:11–12, we find:

JUDGES 6:11–12
> 11 There came *an* angel of the Lord, and sat under an oak which was in Ophrah, that pertained unto Joash the Abiezrite: and his son Gideon threshed wheat by the wine press, to hide it from the Midianites.
> 12 And *the* angel of the Lord appeared unto him, and said unto him, The Lord is with thee, thou mighty man of valour.

The same angel is referred to both ways in this passage: *an* angel of the Lord and *the* angel of the Lord. You can't say "*an* angel of the Lord" means only an angel that God sent, and "*the* angel of the Lord" means Jesus.

Therefore, you can't make a doctrine out of the articles "a," "an," or "the." It doesn't work. It's a poor way to make doctrine, because it doesn't withstand the test of scripture.

Notice the Jews didn't thresh their wheat on threshing floors any longer, for fear that the Midianites would come looking for it and steal it. Instead, they hid it in places where their enemies wouldn't expect it to be.

Continuing the story in verse 12:

JUDGES 6:12

12 And the angel of the Lord appeared unto him, and said unto him, *The Lord is with thee, thou mighty man of valour.*

God calls things that be not as though they were. He does this for us, too. He called us "holy" while we were still sinners. That helps a person get to the place God wants him, and that's what happened here with Gideon.

At this time of Israel's defeat, Gideon, with his negative attitude, didn't look anything like a person of valor! However, God's words helped him get there in the realm of the mind and fulfill God's purpose with newfound strength. Gideon responded to the angel in verses 13 and 14:

JUDGES 6:13–14

13 Oh my Lord, if the Lord be with us, why then is all this befallen us? and where be all his miracles which our fathers told us of, saying, Did not the Lord bring us up from Egypt? but now the Lord hath forsaken us, and delivered us into the hands of the Midianites.

14 And the Lord looked upon him, and said, Go in this thy might, and thou shalt save Israel from the hand of the Midianites: *have not I sent thee?*

When God sends you somewhere, remember who sent you. Faithfulness is inspired by the fact that you *know* God sent you. That knowledge will keep you steady in that position.

So when God tells you to put your hand to something, do it with joy, knowing He told you to do it. Remembering this will be comforting and faith-building when you come to tests or trials.

GIDEON'S MISGIVINGS

Gideon may have been somewhat reassured when God said He was sending him to deliver the Jewish people, yet think of all the questions

Gideon must have had: "How am I going to do that? I'm just here threshing the wheat—how am I going to save Israel from those powerful oppressors?" He asked:

JUDGES 6:15–18

15 Oh my Lord, wherewith shall I save Israel? behold, my family is poor in Manasseh, and I am the least in my father's house.

16 And the Lord said unto him, Surely I will be with thee, and thou shalt smite the Midianites as one man.

17 And he said unto him, If now I have found grace in thy sight, then *shew me a sign that thou talkest with me.*

18 Depart not hence, I pray thee, until I come unto thee, and bring forth my present, and set it before thee. And he said, I will tarry until thou come again.

I wish some people would be like Gideon and be careful about supernatural experiences. I don't mean you should be unbelieving when they happen to you; just be careful—because *everything supernatural is not from God!*

Gideon wanted something to confirm that this experience was truly God speaking to him, and that's not such a bad attitude. However, when he asked for three confirmations in a row later on, that might be considered a little on the side of unbelief.

The "Angel" Accepts the Sacrifice

God said things to Gideon that comforted and strengthened him. Gideon went in and prepared a sacrifice, then came outside and offered it to "the angel of the Lord," the Lord Himself.

There is no angel sent from God other than this angel, "the angel of the Lord"—the Lord Himself—who would *ever* receive an offering or a sacrifice. The other angels of God would never even permit a human being to begin to make an offering to them. This angel, however, received the offering. That proves who He was!

JUDGES 6:20–21

20 And the angel of God said unto him, Take the flesh and the unleavened cakes, and lay them upon this rock, and pour out the broth. And he did so.

21 Then the angel of the Lord put forth the end of the staff that was in his hand, and touched the flesh and the unleavened cakes; and there rose up fire out of the rock, and consumed the flesh and the unleavened cakes. Then the angel of the Lord departed out of his sight.

Fire doesn't normally come from rocks, does it? "The angel of the Lord" received that offering supernaturally, and He departed supernaturally. From this you can see that it was God Who appeared to Gideon that day—there's no doubt about it.

GOD REVEALS HIS PLAN

God had a plan, and He revealed it to Gideon step by step. When God starts to reveal His plan for you, you won't know what the second step is until you take the first.

You may think that Gideon was somewhat unbelieving in the way he took some of these steps, but Gideon wasn't acting in unbelief. Faith was rising in him because of what God had said to him, and he was doing the best he could with what he knew.

You know much more than he did, and you know that God doesn't want you to set out fleeces, like Gideon did later in chapter 6. *Those who live by fleeces will get fleeced today!* Gideon was learning as he went, and he didn't have the revelation believers in this dispensation have.

Did God act as a Deliverer of Israel when He walked this earth in the person of Jesus Christ? Surely He did. When He commissioned His disciples, He told them to cast out devils, and they did. What did He say in the Great Commission? The same thing: *"In my name shall they cast out devils"* (Mark 16:17).

Is that the only way deliverance comes? No, deliverance also comes from walking in the truth. God is our Deliverer, and in His Word He tells us how to be delivered.

PARTAKING OF YOUR INHERITANCE

In Colossians, there is a passage that has to do with the Early Church and also with believers today. It tells what God has done for you and how you must continually walk in the light of this knowledge to receive it.

COLOSSIANS 1:12
12 Giving thanks unto the Father, which hath made us meet to be partakers of the inheritance of the saints in light.

God has made you able to partake of your spiritual inheritance, and this is part of it:

COLOSSIANS 1:13
13 Who hath delivered us from the power of darkness, and hath translated us into the kingdom of his dear Son.

If you understand that one statement—if you get that revelation into your heart—you will never again be troubled by anything the enemy does!

DELIVERANCE IS YOURS!

Jesus has already delivered you! Some people walk around behaving like it hasn't happened yet. They act like they are trying to do what Jesus already did. But He *has* delivered you from the power of darkness; and He *has* translated you into the kingdom of His dear Son, which is *"far above all principality, and power, and might, and dominion, and every name that is named,"* as Paul writes in Ephesians 1:21.

Jesus has done the work of deliverance, and you need to *receive* it. The Word of God tells you not only how to receive it, but also how to partake over and over again of your inheritance. God *has* delivered His people!

As He walked the earth, Jesus constantly delivered those who were oppressed of the devil. You can see it throughout the Gospels. Over and over again, Jesus cast spirits out of people with His Word, and He taught them how to walk in the Word to stay free from that kind of problem.

Hebrews 2 is the basis for everything Jesus did:

HEBREWS 2:14
14 For as much then as the children are partakers of flesh and blood, he also
   himself likewise took part of the same; that through death he might destroy
   him that had the power of death, that is, the devil.

In His death, burial, and resurrection, Jesus destroyed the devil.
The word "destroyed" doesn't necessarily mean totally done away
with, annihilated, and never to be seen again, however.

What does it mean? It means Jesus cut you and everyone else who
believes in Him loose from Satan's works. He loosened you from that
power that held you in bondage—that power from which man cannot
loosen himself.

He has also delivered you from death, it says in verse 15:

HEBREWS 2:15
15 And deliver them who through fear of death were all their lifetime subject
   to bondage.

Jesus is our Deliverer. He was Israel's Deliverer as He walked the
earth. He was the Deliverer of Israel in the days of Gideon, when He
appeared as "the angel of the Lord."

PROTECTION

Protection goes hand in hand with deliverance. Sometimes it is difficult to tell which is which, but it doesn't matter, because protection
can be another aspect of deliverance. Let's look again at Psalm 34:7:

PSALM 34:7
7 The angel of the Lord encampeth round about them that fear him, and delivereth [or protects] them.

You will find many examples of God's deliverance at times of need
in the Bible.

In the days of Daniel, when Shadrach, Meshach, and Abednego
were cast into Nebuchadnezzar's burning fiery furnace, "the angel of

the Lord" appeared in the furnace with them. Even the heathen king Nebuchadnezzar said:

DANIEL 3:25
25 Lo, I see four men loose, walking in the midst of the fire, and they have no hurt; and *the form of the fourth man* is like the Son *of God.*

When even an ungodly man like the king could see that, it must have been pretty obvious!

"The angel of the Lord" Himself appeared to deliver these men because of the stand they took and its importance to the nation of Israel at that time.

The Jews were in Babylonian captivity because they didn't believe God, yet here were three men who demonstrated what would happen if they did believe: God Himself would appear and keep His Word—as He did for these men. They were unharmed, and not even the smell of smoke remained on their bodies or their garments.

When Daniel was thrown into the lions' den and emerged unscathed the following morning, he told King Darius:

DANIEL 7:22
22 My God hath sent his angel, and hath shut the lions' mouths.

The Lord appeared in that day, and He is still protecting believers today. Have you been protected? Have you been delivered from situations? God's Word works, and it works for believers today. God's deliverance and protection work hand in hand. You don't need to be afraid of anything. God is with you, and He will keep His Word to you!

INTERCESSION

As Jesus appeared on the earth, He made intercession for men at different times. He came into the earth to do that. Some will wonder, "Why didn't He do it in Heaven?" Because of the covenant and the time in which He appeared.

He came to earth Himself to make intercession, and today He has a Body in the earth, the Body of Christ, the Church. That Body prays and makes intercession as He leads it.

The Lord will also make intercession for you in Heaven, as we will see, but the Body is here. He doesn't have to come back and forth all the time to make intercession anymore, because of a greater covenant founded on greater promises. Today He is dwelling in His Body. Under the Old Covenant, however, He had to appear in person to do certain things.

The first chapter of Zechariah tells about a vision the prophet Zechariah had. He saw unusual things that needed to be explained. In Zechariah chapter 1 verse 9, he said:

ZECHARIAH 1:9
9   Then said I, O my lord, what are these? And *the angel* that talked with me said unto me, I will shew thee what these be.

Notice that an angel was talking with him. That's all it says about the angel at this moment. With just that much information, you wouldn't know whether it was "the angel of the Lord" or not. Angels that were not "the angel of the Lord" have talked with people before and since.

A VISION OF "THE ANGEL OF THE LORD"

Zechariah 1:10–16 says:

ZECHARIAH 1:10–16
10   And the man that stood among the myrtle trees answered and said, These are they whom the Lord hath sent to walk to and fro through the earth.
11   And they answered the angel of the Lord that stood among the myrtle trees, and said, We have walked to and fro through the earth, and, behold, all the earth sitteth still, and is at rest.
12   Then the angel of the Lord answered and said, O Lord of hosts, how long wilt thou not have mercy on Jerusalem and on the cities of Judah, against which thou hast had indignation these threescore and ten years?
13   And the Lord answered the angel that talked with me with good words and comfortable words.

14 So the angel that communed with me said unto me, Cry thou saying, Thus saith the Lord of hosts: I am jealous for Jerusalem and for Zion with a great jealousy.

15 And I am very sore displeased with the heathen that are at ease: for I was but a little displeased, and they helped forward the affliction.

16 Therefore thus saith the Lord; I am returned to Jerusalem with mercies: my house shall be built in it, saith the Lord of hosts, and a line shall be stretched forth upon Jerusalem.

When the angel said that God's house would be rebuilt, it reveals who that angel was. There wasn't any other angel who had a house in Jerusalem. There is only one Being who has a Temple in Jerusalem: God.

Notice what the angel of the Lord did in this passage. He prayed. It was God the Son praying with God the Father about mercy coming to Jerusalem. The Son came into the earth and made intercession with His Father for God's covenant people.

That wasn't some kind of an exercise; it was necessary in that day, because God's covenant people did not yet understand how to do such a thing themselves. Jesus came to intercede for them because of their faith in God, and He made intercession for them to be delivered from their captivity and return to their homeland.

THE LORD'S PRAYER

We traditionally call Matthew 6:9–15, where Jesus taught His disciples how to pray, the Lord's Prayer. However, if there is such a thing as the *Lord's* Prayer in the Bible, I believe it is found in John chapter 17.

If you read John 17 carefully, you will find that the Lord is making intercession for believers in this chapter, asking for things we would have need of—and God gave Him everything He asked for! For example, Jesus prayed:

JOHN 17:17

17 Sanctify them through thy truth: thy word is truth.

Jesus interceded much of the time He walked the earth. He often sent His disciples across the Sea of Galilee while He prayed on a nearby mountaintop.

What do you suppose He was praying about? He made repeated intercession for His disciples. In some instances, he prayed for them to cross the Sea of Galilee safely in the midst of a storm. Overcoming in times of trial brings opportunities to grow in the knowledge of God.

In Hebrews 7:22, we read:

HEBREWS 7:22
22 By so much was Jesus made a surety of a better testament.

Jesus is the surety or guarantee of the better testament, the New Covenant. This means He is the assurance or the insurance of it. He is what gives you confidence that you can trust it. You know the covenant will be kept, because Jesus is the surety of it.

Jesus' part in the New Covenant is found in the following verses:

HEBREWS 7:23–25
23 And they truly were many priests, because they were not suffered to continue by reason of death:
24 But this man [Jesus], because he continueth ever, hath an unchangeable priesthood.
25 Wherefore he is able also to save them to the uttermost that come unto God by him, seeing *he ever liveth to make intercession for them.*

JESUS INTERCEDES FOR YOU!

Jesus is making intercession for you! The next time you get in a hard place, think about that: Jesus is praying for *you!* He will probably touch someone on the earth who is part of His Body—someone with authority in the earth—to pray for you, too. However, His authority is in you as well, because He lives in you.

In Zechariah, we saw Jesus making intercession for His people as "the angel of the Lord." In John 17, we saw Him making intercession for His followers in the days He walked on the earth. And today He continues to make intercession for believers.

ADVOCACY

Jesus is your Advocate (or lawyer) before God. He appears in the presence of God for you. Could you ever have a better lawyer than Jesus? He'll win your case!

"Well, my case might be impossible," you say. It might seem impossible to you, but it's not impossible to God. *With God all things are possible.* If you believe, all things are possible to you.

If the devil comes and accuses you of something, Jesus Christ and His righteousness will be your Advocate.

The Book of Zechariah contains another example of Jesus' appearing on the earth as "the angel of the Lord." He came to make intercession for Joshua, the High Priest.

ZECHARIAH 3:1

1 And he shewed me Joshua the high priest standing before the angel of the Lord, and Satan standing at his right hand to resist him.

Joshua the High Priest was obviously on the earth at that time. He wasn't standing in Heaven or somewhere else—no doubt he was in Jerusalem—as the Jews were rebuilding the Temple there, and he was about to be reinstated and reconsecrated as High Priest.

"Satan standing at his right hand to resist him." Whenever you do anything in obedience to God, you can expect resistance, because Satan is your adversary.

ZECHARIAH 3:2

2 And the Lord said unto Satan, The Lord rebuke thee, O Satan; even the Lord that hath chosen Jerusalem rebuke thee: is not this a brand plucked out of the fire?

In other words, isn't the High Priest a righteous man in the sight of God? This man, Joshua, was standing before "the angel of the Lord." Satan was also standing there. "The angel of the Lord" spoke to the devil and rebuked him.

ZECHARIAH 3:3–4

3 Now Joshua was clothed with filthy garments [his own righteousness], and stood before the angel.

4 And he answered and spake unto those that stood before him, saying, Take away the filthy garments from him. And unto him he said, Behold, *I have caused thine iniquity to pass from thee,* and I will clothe thee with change of raiment.

This tells you who is speaking, doesn't it? Who else but God can remove someone's iniquity?

ADVOCATE OF THE DISCIPLES

Today this Advocate of the disciples is our Advocate, too. In John 17, Jesus prayed for the disciples. In First John 2:1, the Spirit of God said through John:

1 JOHN 2:1

1 My little children, these things write I unto you, that ye sin not.

The Word of God was written for this purpose. Nowhere does the Word of God ever encourage people to walk in sin—never! It says, "God forbid!" These things were written so people would not sin.

1 JOHN 2:1–2

1 And if any man sin, *we have an advocate* with the Father, Jesus Christ the righteous:

2 And *he is the propitiation for our sins:* and not for ours only, but also for the sins of the whole world.

The phrase "He is the propitiation for our sins" means that what Jesus did satisfied God. Jesus' holy, just, and righteous nature fully satisfied His Father. And because He fully satisfied God, you can be fully satisfied in Him, because He satisfies both God and man.

Jesus satisfies man's need to be able to stand boldly in the presence of God, knowing he has been made the righteousness of God in Christ. He satisfied the need of God's holy, just, and righteous nature before man, to enable man to stand in His presence.

Even though the process of holiness, redemption, and sanctification is still being fulfilled or completed in your life, you can stand boldly before God because of Jesus, because you are standing in *His* righteousness. He is your Advocate, and He will win your case—always, always, always!

JUDGMENT

Jesus also acts in ways to bring the judgment of God's Word to pass.

In Second Kings 19:35–37, we saw that "the angel of the Lord" appeared in the Assyrian camp one night and smote 185,000 men who agreed with their king in blaspheming, "God can't deliver you, Israel." He executed judgment on them so deliverance could come to the Jews.

Enoch prophesied, according to Jude 14 and 15, that the Lord would come with ten thousand of His saints to execute judgment upon all who are ungodly. And as He walked on this earth, Jesus spoke words that brought judgment upon people who stood in opposition to the path of righteousness. He will do so again as He did in that day.

CONFIRMS THE COVENANT

The angel of the Lord confirmed the covenant when He appeared to Abraham in Ur of the Chaldees, preached the Gospel to him, and made a promise to covenant with him.

As the years went on, He kept that covenant, He brought that covenant to fruition, and He walked through the pieces of the covenant to show Abraham how the Lord would keep the covenant for him as He delivered him.

He instructed Abraham in keeping the covenant to the point where Abraham was so established in that covenant that when the Lord spoke to him and told him to offer his own son as a sacrifice, he was willing to do it! Why? He knew God was able to raise the boy from the dead, because God had promised that in Isaac would the seed be called. That's how much confidence Abraham had in God!

HEBREWS 11:19

19 Accounting that God was able to raise him up, even from the dead; from
whence also he received him in a figure.

Abraham and Sara were both "dead in body" when they met "the
angel of the Lord" and heard His promise of a son. In other words,
they were well past childbearing years, but God gave Sarah strength
to conceive and carry Isaac (verses 11 and 12).

God meant no harm to come to Isaac, yet Abraham was willing
to sacrifice him. That gave God authority to give His Son to this
world for salvation. Because Abraham was willing to give his son to
God, God could give His only begotten Son to mankind. Abraham
was blessed, and God continually confirmed that covenant with him
throughout Abraham's life.

COMMUNION AND COVENANT

Does God do that for you? Every time you take Communion, He is
confirming the New Covenant He made in Christ through His blood
and His Body for your redemption. You do not need to wait for Communion to have God confirm the covenant. All you need to do is take
a step of faith. Every time you do, God confirms the covenant. He
keeps His Word; He watches over His Word to perform it; thereby He
confirms the covenant.

COMFORT

Why is the Holy Spirit called the Comforter? Because He *comforts*
us, and He is a wonderful Comforter!

In Genesis chapter 16, you will find where the second member of
the Godhead came to the earth to comfort a person.

Do you remember how Abram and Sarai (as they were called then)
got impatient and tried to make God's covenant come to pass on their
own? Sarai had the bright idea of allowing Abram to father a child by
her maid, Hagar. The result was Ishmael—but Ishmael was not the
promised child!

You can't make God's word happen.

Once Hagar was pregnant, she became rather cocky about it, because she was pregnant and Sarai wasn't. Sarai found that her maid now despised her, and when Sarai dealt harshly with her, Hagar fled into the wilderness.

The wilderness was the wrong place to run, but God did not forsake Hagar. She really wasn't responsible for her situation; Abraham and Sarai were. Hagar was their servant, and she had to do whatever they said.

COMFORT FOR A RUNAWAY

Genesis 16:7–9 says:

GENESIS 16:7–9

7 *And the angel of the Lord found her* by a fountain of water in the wilderness.

8 And he said, Hagar, Sarai's maid, whence camest thou? and whither wilt thou go? And she said, I flee from the face of my mistress Sarai.

9 *And the* angel *of the* Lord said unto her, Return to thy mistress, and submit thyself under her hands.

"The angel of the Lord" went after her. Do you see that? He advised her to return home. What God tells us to do will bring comfort to us if we will do it. This is what He told Hagar:

GENESIS 16:10–11

10 And the angel of the Lord said unto her, I will multiply thy seed exceedingly, that it shall not be numbered for multitude.

11 And *the angel of the Lord said* unto her, Behold, thou art with child, and shalt bear a son, and shalt call his name Ishmael; *because the Lord hath heard thy affliction.*

"The angel of the Lord" found her out in the wilderness, and He comforted her. Do you think it helped? You know it helped. She did what He told her to do, and she returned home. She had Ishmael, and God blessed her son, as Abraham asked Him to. As much as it was possible for God to do, He blessed the boy abundantly.

COMFORT FOR THE DISCIPLES

As Jesus walked the earth, He often comforted His disciples, and as He lives in you today, He is doing the same thing. He is your Comforter.

When people are grieved or troubled, the Word of God says you can comfort them with the comfort with which you have been comforted (2 Cor. 1:4). That's true. I've seen it happen in my own life in many ways and on many occasions.

God can use you to comfort others when they are hurting, afflicted, destitute, or grieving for a loved one. He will comfort them with the same comfort that is in you—the comfort with which He has comforted you.

COMFORT FOR THE HEALED

Jesus also comforted the man who was born blind. As you know, the Pharisees were going to stone Jesus to death, but He walked away through the midst of them (John 8:59).

While He was walking away, He found this man who was born blind. He stopped and ministered to him, and the man was healed.

Picture it: The Pharisees were standing around still holding their stones while Jesus was laying hands on the blind man. Suddenly the man's eyes were opened, and he received his sight! All the Pharisees did was give him a hard time, and his parents didn't even back him up.

Then, in John chapter 9, the Pharisees asked the man again:

JOHN 9:26–33

26 What did he do to thee? how opened he thine eyes?

27 He answered them, I have told you already, and ye did not hear: wherefore would ye hear it again? will ye also be his disciples?

28 Then they reviled him, and said, Thou art his disciple; but we are Moses' disciples.

29 We know that God spake unto Moses: as for this fellow, we know not from whence he is.

30 The man answered and said to them, Why herein is a marvellous thing, that ye know not from whence he is, and yet he hath opened mine eyes.

31 Now we know that God heareth not sinners: but if any man be a worshipper of God, and doeth his will, him he heareth.

32 Since the world began was it not heard that any man opened the eyes of one that was born blind.

33 If this man were not of God, he could do nothing.

RELIGION'S RESPONSE

The former blind man was getting bolder by the minute, and the Pharisees were getting madder at him and giving him a harder time by the minute.

Instead of rejoicing with him that his eyes were opened and he could see for the first time in his life, they were persecuting him for it! Religion does that.

JOHN 9:34–38

34 They answered and said unto him, Thou wast altogether born in sins, and dost thou teach us? And they cast him out.

35 Jesus heard that they had cast him out; and when he had found him, he said unto him, Dost thou believe on the Son of God?

36 He answered and said, Who is he, Lord, that I might believe on him?

37 And Jesus said unto him, Thou hast both seen him, and it is he that talketh with thee.

38 And he said, Lord, I believe. And he worshipped him.

Jesus found the blind man and further revealed Himself to him. The man didn't just get healed that day; he got saved!

Jesus did that several other times when people got healed, and the religious leaders gave them a hard time. He found them and taught them, because they would be confused about healing and salvation if someone didn't explain what had happened to them.

They might think, "Jesus healed me, but everyone is mad. Should I feel bad because I'm healed? Maybe it wasn't the will of God for me to be healed."

The Lord will seek you out when you need comfort, too, just like He sought out Hagar in the wilderness and this man in the Temple.

JESUS THROUGH THE AGES

In this chapter, we have seen the parallels of the ministry of Christ Jesus in us today by His Spirit, Jesus as He walked this earth, and with the ministry of "the angel of the Lord" (found in times before Christ's incarnation, but nonetheless Jesus appearing to His covenant people).

In all three of these cases, we see the Word of God being kept, the will of God being done or accomplished in response to man's faith, and the love of God being manifested to His people. Jesus Christ the same yesterday, today, and forever. Amen.

As I close this account of God's Word and angelic ministry, I am greatly impressed to give thanks to God for what He has provided for us. In this life in an alien world, God has given us the victory over the world, the flesh, and the devil.

Thank You, Father, for You have truly done all things well. Thank you for making us believers able to partake of our inheritance and overcome fully in Christ our Lord.

"What should I do with my life?"

If you've been asking yourself this question, **RHEMA BIBLE TRAINING COLLEGE is a good place to come and find out.** RBTC will build a solid biblical foundation in you that will carry you through—wherever life takes you.

The Benefits:

◆ Training at *the* **top Spirit-filled Bible school**

◆ Teaching based on steadfast faith in God's Word

◆ Unique two-year core program specially designed to **grow** you as a believer, help you **recognize the voice of God**, and equip you to **live successfully**

◆ Optional **specialized training** in the third- and fourth-year program of your choice: Biblical Studies, Helps Ministry, Itinerant Ministry, Pastoral Ministry, Student Ministries, Worship, World Missions, and General Extended Studies

◆ **Accredited** with Transworld Accrediting Commission International

◆ Worldwide **ministry opportunities**— while you're in school

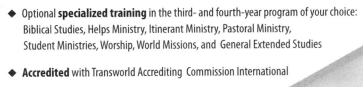

Apply today!
1-888-28-FAITH (1-888-283-2484)
rbtc.org

Always on.

For the latest news and information on products, media, podcasts, study resources, and special offers, visit us online 24 hours a day.

Free Subscription!

Call now to receive a free subscription to *The Word of Faith* magazine from Kenneth Hagin Ministries. Receive encouragement and spiritual refreshment from . . .

- *Faith-building articles from Kenneth W. Hagin, Lynette Hagin, Craig W. Hagin, Denise Hagin Burns, and others*

- *"Timeless Teaching" from the archives of Kenneth E. Hagin*

- *Feature articles on prayer and healing*

- *Testimonies of salvation, healing, and deliverance*

- *Children's activity page*

- *Updates on Rhema Bible Training College, Rhema Bible Church, and other outreaches of Kenneth Hagin Ministries*

Subscribe today for your free *Word of Faith*!

1-888-28-FAITH (1-888-283-2484)

rhema.org/wof